Conflict Management for Security Professionals

M000232732

Conflict Management for Security Professionals

Andrew A. Tufano

AMSTERDAM • BOSTON • HEIDELBERG • LONDON • NEW YORK • OXFORD
PARIS • SAN DIEGO • SAN FRANCISCO • SINGAPORE • SYDNEY • TOKYO
Butterworth-Heinemann is an imprint of Elsevier

ELSEVIER

Acquiring Editor: Brian Romer
Senior Editorial Project Manager: Amber Hodge
Project Manager: Punithavathy Govindaradjane
Designer: Matthew Limbert

Butterworth-Heinemann is an imprint of Elsevier
225 Wyman Street, Waltham, MA 02451, USA
The Boulevard, Langford Lane, Kidlington, Oxford, OX5 1 GB, UK

Notices
Knowledge and best practice in this field are constantly changing. As new research
and experience broaden our understanding, changes in research methods or professional practices,
may become necessary. Practitioners and researchers must always rely on their own experience
and knowledge in evaluating and using any information or methods described herein. In using such
information or methods they should be mindful of their own safety and the safety of others, including
parties for whom they have a professional responsibility.

To the fullest extent of the law, neither the Publisher nor the authors, contributors, or editors, assume any
liability for any injury and/or damage to persons or property as a matter of products liability, negligence
or otherwise, or from any use or operation of any methods, products, instructions, or ideas contained in
the material herein.

Library of Congress Cataloging-in-Publication Data
Tufano, Andrew A.
  Conflict management for security professionals / Andrew A. Tufano.
    pages cm
  Includes bibliographical references and index.
  ISBN 978-0-12-417196-1 (alk. paper)
  1. Private security services. 2. Police, Private. 3. Conflict management. I. Title.
  HV8290.T84 2014
  363.28'90684—dc23   2013027247

British Library Cataloguing-in-Publication Data
A catalogue record for this book is available from the British Library.

ISBN: 978-0-12-417196-1

Printed and bound in the United States of America

14 15 16 17 18   10 9 8 7 6 5 4 3 2 1

  **Working together
to grow libraries in
developing countries**

www.elsevier.com • www.bookaid.org

For information on all Butterworth–Heinemann publications
visit our website at store.elsevier.com

Contents

Section II   Policies

Section III   People as Part of a Conflict Resolution Strategy

Section IV   Implementing Conflict Resolution Strategies

Acknowledgments

No one works alone or accomplishes anything of real value without the significant support of others. I would like to thank a number of people who directly or indirectly assisted with this work.

First, I want to thank my wife Cindy, who has "put up with me" while working on this project. There were many long nights and several occasions when I wanted to quit, and she was there to reassure me that the ideas that I was writing about were important and needed to be heard.

Next, I need to thank Henrie Watkins for the many hours he spent with me trying to "save the world"! I need to thank another friend, Mariusz Ozminkowski, a wonderful writer who encouraged me to finish my manuscript. I also want to thank Scott Martin, a friend and pioneer in the healthcare security industry, who has contributed more to this project and my life than he could ever know.

Additionally, I am grateful to countless other unnamed security professionals and friends who have been sounding boards for many of my ideas and have challenged me to think more deeply about them.

Finally, I would like to thank my father for paving the way. In this case the apple fell close to the tree!

"Either write something worth reading or do something worth writing."
—Ben Franklin

My attempt!

About the Author

Andrew Tufano has worked in the security industry for over 25 years. He holds a master's degree from California State University at Fullerton. Over the past 25 years, Andrew has been employed in various senior security positions, including security company owner (PPO), security trainer, and security consultant. He holds various security industry weapons instructor and end-user certifications. He is an active member of the International Association for Healthcare Security & Security (IAHSS).

Andrew has created several business ventures, including Goldstar Security LLC, Goldstar Tactical Training, and the Force Decisions Institute. He is an industry-recognized expert in private-person use of force. Andrew is currently an adjunct professor and experienced college educator at a public southern California college.

The author is available to present this material for seminars, training sessions, or conferences. He can be reached at andy@forcedecisions.com.

Inspiration

I've always been fascinated by the way people dealt with interpersonal field conflict. As I grew up in a law enforcement family, my father, brother (both police officers), and I had numerous conversations about violence and how first responders deal with conflict. (I now continue these conversations with my police officer son.) Our early conversations focused on police officers who seemingly used excessive physical force to subdue resistant suspects and came under scrutiny, whereas other talks involved police officers who used inadequate levels of physical force and paid for it with their lives.[1] Often the officers involved in these conflicts were harshly criticized by the public and their agencies; some were fired. These discussions made it clear to me that first responders have an extremely difficult job deciding the "best" conflict resolution strategy to apply when faced with intense and highly fluid interpersonal field conflict.

Later in our lives, as the three of us transitioned into the private security market (while my son transitioned from the security field to the law enforcement industry), all of us continued to discuss our own unique conflict resolution challenges.

Although there are great distinctions between the law enforcement community and the private security industry, these two industries have at least one thing in common: their personal and corporate success depends on how well they manage and resolve interpersonal field conflict.

The Bottom Line

To resolve conflict and maintain safe organizations, professional security personnel need access to a full spectrum of conflict resolution strategies.

Process

I continue to be perplexed by stakeholders who are convinced that it's possible to maintain high levels of organizational safety without the need to employee

---

[1] On January 16, 1998, Deputy Kyle Dinkheller of the Laurens County Sheriff's Office was shot and killed after conducting a traffic stop on a rural road about six miles north of Dublin, Georgia. Dinkheller attempted to gain control of a violent, mentally deranged suspect using his verbal tactics training, but he failed. The entire incident was videotaped by Deputy Dinkheller's patrol car video system.

professionally trained security personnel who have access to a full range of conflict resolution strategies.

Over the past 25 years I've been involved in thousands of interpersonal field conflict interactions while employed in the capacity of uniformed security officer, plainclothes shoplifter agent, security trainer, security consultant, and security company owner. I can personally attest to the fact that to safely resolve interpersonal field conflict and protect individuals, security personnel need access to a multitude of conflict resolution options beyond simply "observing and reporting."

Communication Solutions

My personal frustrations of trying to find the perfect approach for resolving interpersonal conflict led me to earn a graduate degree in communication. I was assured by many intelligent people that talk was the best conflict resolution solution and a useful substitution for physical conflict resolution strategies. This "conflict resolution through communication" approach suggests that with the right quantity and quality of communication, uncooperative individuals could be persuaded, without the need to use physical force, to correct their behavior. The underlying premise for this communicative solution is the belief that if public safety personnel (the communicators) were more patient and understanding with uncooperative subjects, those subjects would be more likely to peacefully submit to those in authority. Negative field conflict outcomes, they argue, is primarily the result of misapplied communication tactics and a lack of self-control on the security individual's part, which in turn exacerbates (or creates) interpersonal resistance.

Some believe that security personnel self-discipline is the key to helping uncooperative subjects understand the error of their ways, thus creating in them the necessary motivation for a change in behavior. Unfortunately, conflict resolution strategies that primarily focus on communication tactics, while minimizing or dismissing the role of force or protective action, are ineffective, or worse; they create a false sense of safety and don't provide protection for employees and community members.

History has taught us that no matter how well-trained public safety personnel become in the various forms of communication tactics, there are still some violent individuals that cannot be reasoned with and need to be physically constrained from harming community members. There is and always will be a percentage of conflict that can't be peacefully resolved with just talk. Unfortunately, even those stakeholders that affirm this truth[2] still don't trust their own security personnel to effectively use physical conflict resolution strategies to successfully resolve field conflict.

---

[2] See Chapter 6 for a more detailed exposition of conflict and violence.

These stakeholders don't see the business value of allowing their security personnel to physically intervene to resolve field conflict, but instead rely on the police.

The Reality of Violence

Over the years of studying the ongoing battles between uncooperative, dangerous, and violent individuals and private security personnel, I've learned the ugly truth that many are still uncomfortable acknowledging: No forceless policy can effectively resolve conflict, protect people, and maintain safe and secure organizations.

Every business today is faced with the inevitability, unavoidability, and unpredictability of conflict. Unfortunately, when conflict is not properly managed, it creates unsafe environments, physical injuries, property loss and damage, and increases in civil liability, and it tarnishes an organization's reputation. The bottom line is that failure to effectively manage and resolve conflict impedes an organization's ability to maintain financial stability.

Better Suited

There are many reasons an organization's own security personnel are better situated to resolve field conflict than "responding" law enforcement officers. The most obvious benefit is their ability to respond to the scene faster than the police. When people are being victimized, waiting for help to arrive is rarely preferred over being helped by on-scene Good Samaritans. Even under perfect circumstances, it could take police officers up to eight minutes or more to arrive at the scene of a serious incident[3] (Eberly).

Invention

The primary reason I wrote this book was that I noticed a great deal of confusion in the security industry and among many organizations as to how best to utilize security personnel in the conflict resolution process. Unfortunately, in many instances security personnel are thought of as part of the *problem,* not the solution! As I've surveyed the industry, I've found that no consistent conflict resolution standard or overriding philosophy guides the security industry or many of my clients. One noted exception is found in the healthcare industry.[4]

---

[3]Current police agency budgetary constraints may also create a much longer wait time for service in some areas.

[4]MAB, MOAB, PMAB, and CPI are systematic, low-risk broad-based communicative conflict resolution programs found in the healthcare and hospital industry.

To meet the unique challenges of healthcare settings, and due in large part to statutory and regulatory healthcare requirements (which are rare in other security/safety contexts), a broad-based communicative conflict resolution system[5] was developed to deal with passive-aggressive individuals during the initial contact stage of customer service complaints. However, these conflict resolution strategies become less effective (or ineffective) once an individual's behavior escalates from passive aggressive to directly aggressive and/or in secondary stages of interpersonal contact.[6] Escalation in conflict behavior is usually the impetus for "calling security." When first-responder security or police personnel arrive at the scene of a conflict, it has usually escalated beyond passive aggressiveness to either direct aggression or actual violence. Unlike those who were initially involved at the early stages of interpersonal field conflict, the responding personnel are met with a very different set of interpersonal field conflict resolution dynamics.[7] Conflict resolution techniques (e.g., verbal tactics) that may have initially worked are ineffective at the secondary contact phase of interpersonal field conflict. These changing dynamics are the primary reason that attempts to use initial contact or passive-aggressive behavior conflict resolution strategies usually fail when they're applied by security personnel to higher levels of interpersonal field conflict. "Communication-only" conflict resolution strategies are typically only effective at the initial contact phase and when dealing with passive-aggressive individuals.

The truth is, when communication fails, the only way to safely resolve conflict is for professionally trained personnel to physically intervene as quickly as possible. Unfortunately, many senior stakeholders and those involved in creating these conflict resolution programs fail to understand this basic conflict resolution axiom.

The Law of Probabilities

Organizational safety is one of the most important challenges facing the 21st-century business community. Unfortunately, many organizations don't take conflict resolution seriously. Clients have told me many times that the reason they don't want to invest in security personnel (or security resources) is that there's very little chance that anything bad will happen. Unfortunately, the use of probability is often a faulty predictor of risk! The "low probability" of a violent incident happening has been shown time and time again to be a poor indicator of predicting

---

[5] These verbal techniques are used by a wide variety of employee types and in various interpersonal contexts. However, they're not specifically geared toward the type of interpersonal conflict that security personnel have to deal with, including resolving field conflict with violent individuals.

[6] We distinguish between those who initially make contact with uncooperative subjects and those who are called in "after the fact" to assist with conflict resolution.

[7] Interpersonal field conflict dynamics are covered in more detail in Chapter 10.

actual violence.[8] This miscalculation creates a false sense of safety for many stake-holders and community members. The day before a deranged murderer killed 20 children and 6 adults[9] in Newtown, Connecticut, the Sandy Hook Elementary School administrators and community felt safe.

Even in the wake of all these violent incidents, many organizations are still using probability as a reliable method for determining their potential risk. The "It couldn't possibly happen here" approach to conflict resolution keeps organizations from preparing for the inevitability, unavoidability, and unpredictability of conflict and violence.

There are many unpleasant realities associated with an organization's failure to effectively resolve conflict. They range from losing customers and employees to perceptions that their environment is unsafe to losing customers and employees when they're murdered on an organization's property!

The truth is, most organizations don't really understand the nature of conflict or how to best resolve it without creating unnecessary organizational risk. But worse than this, organizations often exacerbate the problem by "contracting out" conflict resolution rather than dealing with it themselves.

Many organizations avoid being directly involved in attempts to resolve conflict because they falsely believe it's safer and creates less total liability if they leave conflict resolution to their local law enforcement agency. However, organizations that employ professionally trained security personnel who have access to a wide array of conflict resolution strategies are able to efficiently resolve interpersonal field conflict and maintain safe and secure environments.

Recommendations

This book is both a persuasive essay and a practical guide for helping organizations map out the necessary organizational processes for implementing reliable interpersonal field conflict resolution systems. It covers the necessary principles, philosophies, policies, procedures, processes, and personnel needed to develop a reliable field conflict resolution system.[10]

When professional security personnel[11] are trained and authorized to use a full spectrum of conflict resolution strategies to manage and resolve conflict within a reliable conflict resolution system, organizations are able to maintain high levels of organizational safety.

---

[8] See Chapter 6 for a partial list of the most current violent incidents.

[9] Newtown, Connecticut, December 14, 2012.

[10] A reliable conflict resolution system consists of professional personnel, effective processes, and high levels of accountability.

[11] We distinguish professional security personnel from basic security personnel. Professional security personnel are held to high training and operational standards and are held accountable for their actions.

Audience

This book was written with two primary audiences in mind:

1. Senior *nonsecurity* organizational stakeholders who are directly or indirectly responsible for or have influence or oversight over their organization's security function
2. Dedicated and frustrated security professionals who are personally involved in managing and resolving field conflict and protecting organizational and community members

"Protect and Serve"

Successful organizations "protect" their people, property, and reputation while "serving" their consumer needs. Effective conflict resolution is the key to protecting and serving. In the pursuit of "risk-free" organizational safety, some organizations have *neutered* their security personnel or have turned to technological solutions. Our proposed solution will require a paradigm shift away from noninvolvement and toward responsible private security involvement. (This is especially true for organizations that already utilize security personnel in the conflict resolution process.) This change will require *active* participation and cooperative partnerships with senior nonsecurity stakeholders, corporate executives, attorneys, risk managers, human resource managers, police managers, and other influential organizational stakeholders. It will take every vested stakeholder to create the safest and most secure organizations possible.

Underlying Principles of Organizational Conflict Resolution

Chapter 1

Introduction

Successful businesses perform many important organizational tasks, but few are more important than "protecting and serving" their customers and employees. An organization's ability to successfully resolve conflict is a key to that organization's financial and social success. The truth is, organizations cannot maintain financially viability if they are perceived as *unsafe*. Regardless of how great an organization's product or service, it's impossible to compete in any market if customers or employees are at risk.

In an attempt to create safe environments, organizations continue to experiment with various organizational safety philosophies and conflict resolution strategies. Many businesses have created reasonably safe organizations but are still plagued with nagging and recurring safety concerns and are one violent interaction away from an organizational disaster. Poorly managed violent encounters create unsafe conditions and compromise an organization's good will.

Even organizations that have successfully performed many of these safety tasks well have overlooked, perhaps subconsciously, their most important and necessary organizational safety concern:

How to minimize organizational risk associated with uncooperative, danger-ous or violent individuals who create unsafe conditions and interfere with an organization's primary mission.

3

Although there are many *other* important safety related questions that should be asked and solutions proposed, our book focuses on the interpersonal processes associated with the conflict resolution strategies that professional security personnel use to protect people and property and maintain high levels of organizational safety.

Organizations—or more rightly, senior organizational stakeholders—have legal, ethical, and pragmatic reasons for creating safe environments for the people who frequent their organizations' physical boundaries. Although there are various organizational processes and stakeholder activities that influence the formation of safe environments, professional security personnel play a powerful role in the maintenance of organizational safety. However, because most organizations lack a reliable conflict resolution system that efficiently guides their personnel's actions as well as lacking effective leadership, even organizations that employ security personnel often fail to maximize their potential.

Private security personnel are rarely used to their fullest potential because they're typically "untrained and constrained."

The truth is that it's impossible to create high levels of organizational safety unless trained security personnel, who are given responsible behavioral boundaries, are allowed to intervene to resolve conflict. Although some argue that intervention may increase organizational risk, the total liabilities associated with "doing nothing" are much greater than acting. When personnel are acting to protect individuals from harm, it's much easier to defend action than inaction by personnel.

Unfortunately, even those organizations that allow security personnel the option of using protective action make the mistake of allowing its use independent of a comprehensive conflict resolution system. When attempts to resolve conflict go badly, organizations use these negative outcomes as proof that the risks associated with intervention are too high. However, the primary reason for the increases in liability is not because protection action was used but because it was used independently of a comprehensive conflict resolution system. In fact, senior stakeholders often cite "elevated risk" as the reason for prohibiting protective interventions by security personnel. However, when protective action is used within a comprehensive conflict resolution system, risk is mitigated to acceptable levels.

Corporate human resource managers, risk managers, and corporate attorneys often use negative conflict resolution outcomes based on poor decision making as representative examples to affirm their worst suspicions for allowing intervention. For years, a myth has existed (another security industry unexamined assumption) that allowing security personnel the option of using protective action to resolve conflict is always too great an organizational risk. (These assumptions may be true for basic security guards but not for professionally trained security personnel.) In fact, senior stakeholders often use these perceived (or hypothetical) risks to justify outright prohibitions for the use of protective action, restrictive use-of-force limits, and restrictions on the type or kind of protective devices or tools that security personnel are authorized to carry. However, when professional security personnel use the full spectrum of conflict resolution strategies and operate within a comprehensive conflict resolution system, these "self-fulfilling prophecies" rarely come to fruition.

When these operational conditions are met, professional security personnel are extremely effective at maintaining high levels of organizational safety without creating unreasonable organizational risk.

Since organizations are legally and socially *required* to maintain safe environments that provide a *reasonable level* of due care for *anyone* that frequents an organization, including customers, employees, visitors, and many others, the consequences for failing to successfully resolve interpersonal field conflict are legal, financial, and social catastrophes!

The Los Angeles Dodgers found out the hard way. Attorneys for Brian Stow, a fan who was severely beaten at Dodger Stadium in April 2011, report that Stow's medical bills will exceed $50 million! Stow's attorneys filed a lawsuit asking for "punitive damages on top of compensation for the family's losses, contending that … a lack of security constitutes malice, oppression and/or a conscious disregard of the rights and security of Stow" (Kim, 2011). Failing to provide a *responsible* level of *due care* may end up costing the LA Dodgers more than $100 million!

Process

I wrote *Conflict Management for Security Professionals* to support organizations that employ private security personnel; however, these principles also apply to the various *other* ways that organizations manage their individual organizational security programs, such as *ad hoc* security programs, or through contract security services.

Our approach to "protect and serve" goes way beyond simply teaching security personnel various *use-of-force* techniques; it involves the implementation of a reliable and comprehensive conflict resolution system, which includes the underlying organizational protective principles, theories, tactics, and tools that are necessary to effectively manage and resolve conflict.

A comprehensive conflict resolution system should support an organization's *core* organizational safety priorities, such as:

1. Establishing an organizational standard of *acceptable behavior*
2. Enacting legal, administrative, and social *processes* to deal with safety violators
3. Maintaining consistency in the *application of consequences* for safety violators
4. Utilizing *trained* professional security personnel who uphold an organization's organizational safety standard

Since people are naturally selfish and don't like to be told that their behavior is potentially harmful or contrary to an established community standard, organizations need trained and effective professional security personnel, supported by reliable *business-focused* safety principles, to interact with potential safety violators. Whether contrarian behavior is inappropriate or criminal, organizations need *reliable* conflict resolution strategies to keep minor conflict from escalating to violence and to manage and resolve negative interpersonal interactions. Responsible conflict resolution strategies are necessary for helping individuals correct their inappropriate behavior or, in rare instances, to protect individuals from criminal behavior.

The Default Position

Every organization has a "built-in" *default* conflict resolution strategy that may or may not be effective at maintaining organizational safety. This default strategy may involve simply ignoring or placating conflict or conflict makers until the disruption finally becomes so intolerable that someone calls the police. This *reactive* conflict resolution approach is ineffective and unreliable and ultimately creates serious safety concerns for community members. There's too much at stake for an organization's employees and its customers to not have a well thought out and systematic conflict resolution process.

Conflict Management for Security Professionals provides organizations a *blueprint* to create responsible conflict resolution strategies. Included in our book is a reliable, comprehensive, and business-focused conflict resolution system, including an updated private-person *situational protective action risk continuum* (SPARC). Our book was written for organizations that want to provide the highest level of community and personnel safety without increasing potential liabilities or creating obstacles to financial success.

Definitions and Distinctions

Throughout our book we use some words and ideas that may be new to some readers. Early on we identify these terminologies and provide some background and context for our deliberate language choices early on. There are several reasons we use these specific words to describe our ideas. First, these select words are a more precise and a more accurate way to describe these organizational safety processes and the individuals that perform them. Second, we want to use language that clearly distinguishes *private* market organizational safety principles from *public* law enforcement organizational safety philosophies. Finally, we think a change in verbiage is an important component for empowering the *paradigm shift* we're proposing.

For the purpose of our book, *field conflict* is defined as potentially unsafe *interpersonal interactions* between two or more affiliated or nonaffiliated[1] individuals that occur on an organization's property.

Law Enforcement and Private Security Distinctions

One important distinction we need to make is among security and law enforcement *processes, behavior*, and *personnel*. To make these distinctions clear, we need to use certain words or ideas to convey these differences. One of these distinctions is how the phrase *"use of force"* is used and understood. It's true that use-of-force or protective action is used to manage and resolve conflict in both the security and law enforcement communities. However, there are, or should be, distinctions in *how* force is applied in these two contexts. For instance, in the law enforcement industry, *force* is used *primarily* to enforce laws, whereas in the private security industry, force (or protective action) is used (or should be used) *solely* for protection. In fact, when private security personnel attempt to use physical force to enforce laws, rules, or policies, they usually end up creating additional conflict. Therefore, when private security personnel use protective action to resolve interpersonal field conflict, we identify their actions as "protective." We define protective action (used for protective interventions) as:

> *Physical subject contact, whether it's accomplished through personal body contact or with a protective device or tool, for the narrow purpose of protecting individuals (including security personnel, employees or others) from immediate or active physical harm, applied in a manner that minimizes potential injury and maximizes safety for all involved subjects.*

Historical Aspects of Conflict Resolution

Long ago, organizations established their preference for hiring police officers, both active and retired, and in some circumstances former military personnel (both enlisted and commissioned officers), to manage their security needs. There are two basic prevailing thoughts on how this preference became the established hiring pattern for many private organizations. One view suggests that police officers and military personnel are *naturally* safety experts; another view suggests that these individuals

---

[1] We define *affiliated subjects* as those individuals who have a direct relationship to the organization, such as consumers, visitors, or employees, whereas *nonaffiliated subjects* are individuals who have little or no direct relationship with the organization, such as trespassers.

provide a level of *prestige* for the employing organizations. In some cases these benefits and the specific individuals who become employed embody these traits.

However, in many instances these perceived benefits are not actual benefits for organizations.

We've reached this controversial conclusion *not* because these individuals are flawed (they're usually some of the finest people we know) but because of the operational limitations inherent in a private market security setting.

The Setting

There are significant differences between *public* and *private* settings. The *primary* reason our police and military personnel are successful in their respective community safety missions is *not* based on their exemplary personal character, training, or expertise; it's their *enabling authority!* It's true that these individuals typically embody all these traits, and there's no doubt that they play an important role in their *vocational* success, but it's not the primary reason for their success.

In these public settings, task effectiveness is *primarily* the result of authority, *not* an individual's personal character traits.

Military and police personnel are given broad authority and power under state constitutions and the U.S. Constitution, and they enjoy broad societal support for their unique community safety missions. It's true that many of these military and police individuals are of outstanding character, but these character traits are *contributory* factors, not the *primary* reason for their community safety success.

Trials and Tribulations

When police or military-oriented individuals leave their unique employment context and become employed in the private market, they have no more or less authority or power than other individuals who haven't served in the military or those with no police experience. In fact, for some of these individuals, this loss of *social power* is often a source of frustration. Many former police or military individuals have a difficult time making a successful transition from a career with authority, prestige, and power to a job with virtually none. There's a significant *dropout rate* among those who can't adapt to working in a profession with virtually no authority or power. These limitations may give nonpolice/military individuals an advantage over these former public servants, since private personnel can't rely on authority to accomplish their organizational safety mission. Since private security personnel operate under very limited authority, they're forced to find creative, collaborative, and negotiated conflict resolution strategies. Unfortunately, this "limited authority" is sometimes used by security personnel to justify the use of unethical conflict resolution strategies.[2]

The Intended Message of This Book

The truth is there are several unexamined assumptions that guide a private organization's preference for hiring police or military-oriented personnel and for using *public* community safety philosophies. We are *not* saying that police or military experience should be a disqualifying factor for private security employment.

However, we are making a persuasive (and controversial) case that individuals employed for the task of managing and resolving private interpersonal field conflict have the right temperament to process these power inequities and the ambiguity that's a natural part of providing security services in a free market.

The truth is many police *and* military-oriented individuals are not best suited for this type of environment, and *that*'s not their fault. Conversely, very few civilians have the temperament to do *police and military* jobs!

In fact, police departments and the military don't place into field operations newly hired and untested individuals who have no actual experience working in their vocation without first determining whether these recruits have the proper temperament, character, and training to perform these unique tasks. This determination is usually performed by requiring potential candidates to complete a police academy or a military *boot camp*. (The private security industry may benefit from a program designed to determine whether police and military-oriented individuals are able to handle the rigors of the private market.) Likewise, if free-market principles were applied in a police or military context, they would likely fail to produce the desired community safety outcomes. Again, it's not these individuals' fault; rather, it's the natural limitations of private market employment.

To be clear, we admire and appreciate police officers and military personnel. Our society depends on these public heroes (including my own police officer son) to keep us safe. Some of my best friends have worked in both police and military contexts. However, we need to be honest about the unique features and distinctions of the free market and publicly financed enterprises such as police departments and the U.S. military if we are going to make smart *business* decisions for the organizations we represent.

Reference

Kim, V., 2011. Medical costs for bryan stowe to exceed $50 million, attorneys say. LA Now, Los Angeles Times, 13 September 2011; Web: <www.latimesblogs.com> (10.06.12.).

---

[2]See S.A.I.D. in Chapter 4 as one example.

Chapter 2

The "Business-Focused" Community

The Problem

An organization's conflict resolution strategies interfere with its ability to remain profitable, competitive, and socially relevant in its unique business market.

Introduction

The strategies that businesses use to create and maintain safe organizations need to be *natural* extensions of their underlying business philosophy. Unfortunately, safety is often thought of and processed as a separate, standalone, and disintegrated business function that operates outside normative business operating principles.

An effective organizational safety program utilizes business-focused conflict resolution strategies for protecting customers, employees, and visitors from uncooperative, dangerous, and violent individuals who interfere with organizations' ability to remain financially viable in their unique markets. To effectively resolve conflict, organizations need to utilize business-focused organizational safety strategies that easily integrate into their overall business operating philosophy.

11

Although many organizations rely on security personnel to maintain safe and secure environments, security personnel don't have the requisite authority, power, expertise, or training to accomplish this task on their own. Maximizing the collective power of every vested organizational stakeholder provides greater opportunities for maintaining safe organizations and for enhancing an organization's ability to "protect and serve" its customers.

Unfortunately, some organizations continue to experiment with the use of public law enforcement's community safety philosophies that end up exacerbating organizational safety concerns. To effectively integrate private market conflict resolution strategies into an organization's standard business operating processes, law enforcement-based community safety philosophies need to be de-emphasized or replaced with private market organizational safety principles.

Process

Business stakeholders, like security personnel, regularly make multimillion-dollar business decisions. However, unlike business stakeholders, these *business* decisions are not made in the boardroom; they're made in the field every time security personnel interact with uncooperative subjects! In order for security personnel to effectively resolve conflict and act in an organization's best interests, they need to use *business-focused* conflict resolution strategies. Unlike law enforcement-based community safety philosophies, a business-focused approach to conflict resolution empowers security personnel to interact with uncooperative individuals *more like* business stakeholders and *less like* police officers.

Managing Conflict in a Business-Focused Environment

Similar to successful business decision-making processes, organizational conflict resolution problem solving requires a multitude of strategic options. Since the decision to physically interact with an uncooperative subject to resolve conflict is one of the most complicated and important *business* decisions that any stakeholder can make, security personnel need to place a high value on *calculated risk* decision making.[1]

 Many organizations are so obsessed with mitigating use-of-force civil liability that they enact policies that end up ignoring other, more potentially devastating liability, such as negligence associated with a failure to protect their customers, employees, or visitors.

---

[1]Calculated risk takes into consideration the *totality* of risk, not just civil liability claims arising from intervention but additionally from inaction.

To be effective, security personnel need a comprehensive understanding of how the use of, or the failure to use, physical conflict resolution strategies may impact their organization's financial standing. (This exposition needs to go way beyond the well-worn lecture about "… not doing anything to get us sued …..") When inappropriate conflict resolution strategies such as excessive or inadequate physical action are used in a private setting, they impact an organization's ability to remain profitable, competitive, and socially relevant.

ISSUES: DEALING WITH PEOPLE IN A BUSINESS SETTING

Organizations have a legal *duty* to create a safe environment for *anyone* that frequents their jurisdictions. This *due care* responsibility involves creating a safe environment for customers, employees, visitors, and others (including those who have *no* legitimate reason for being present on an organization's property).[2] However, the challenges associated with carrying out this *first duty* are complicated because of an organization's *concurrent* duty to *act reasonably* in carrying out its first duty.

These concurrent duties often confuse stakeholders into thinking that it's better to do nothing rather than act.

To further complicate these organizational safety obligations, organizations don't have an option to not act proactively or reactively to known or should-be-known (foreseeable) safety concerns. Organizations that fail to meet any of these duties create potential civil and criminal negligence. Organizations often interpret these responsibilities as a double-bind dilemma: damned if they do (their duty to act), damned if they don't (their failure to act).

There's no need here to list the thousands of examples in which organizations were sued for negligence. However, one recent example stands out: A female college student sued Southwestern Oregon College Community College and their campus security department for $5 million because she was raped. On the day of the incident, a campus safety officer who was scheduled to work failed to show up for his assigned post, and the post happened to be in proximity to where the student was later raped (Security Law Newsletter). A seemingly basic organizational safety principle of having personnel posted in the community to deter crime may have led to this young woman's injuries and the corresponding lawsuit.

Unfortunately, businesses exacerbate their organizational safety problems by misapplying community safety principles that were created for public police departments. The use of public community safety principles in a private setting creates impediments to organizational safety.

To create the safest organizations possible, it's not enough to simply identify core business-focused conflict resolution principles; it's equally important to point

---

[2] See Chapter 7 for a more detailed exposition.

out competing principles, such as misapplied law enforcement principles, which interfere with private market organizational safety.

Since many private businesses still embrace and utilize public law enforcement safety principles as their guide for organizational safety,[3] here we juxtapose private market organizational safety principles with public law enforcement safety principles and public police officers with private security personnel, to help reinforce and explain the benefits of utilizing business-focused conflict resolution strategies.

Unfortunately, emphasizing private market safety principles and de-emphasizing public law enforcement principles will create some uncomfortable realities with various stakeholder groups.

Because of the high degree of confusion between public law enforcement and private safety principles, it's important for organizations and security personnel to gain a full and comprehensive understanding of these distinctions.

Public law enforcement safety principles are generally ineffective at resolving private market conflict because they're incompatible with standard business operating principles. Law enforcement community safety principles focus on the generalized needs of all organizations located within a specific police jurisdiction (a city, county, or state), whereas private organizational safety principles focus on meeting the needs of one organization—yours!

Although local law enforcement agencies are one of an organization's most important external stakeholder groups and they play an important role in helping individual organizations maintain safe environments, private organizations have very little influence on creating generalized safety outside the boundaries of their organizations. A local law enforcement agency's mission is to support the organizations within its jurisdiction, whereas organizations are responsible for meeting their consumers', employees', and shareholders' needs.

Community members, including organizational stakeholders, have a tendency to conflate private security personnel and police officer roles, whether consciously or unconsciously, because of the perceived similarities of these two groups. This confusion is the basis for many problems noted in the private security industry. Chief among these problems is their inability to maintain high levels of organizational safety without interfering with their organizations' primary business functions. Police officers (and police-oriented individuals) have a propensity for using physicality and enforcement as their primary conflict resolution strategies. Unfortunately, when these strategies are used in a private setting, they interfere with an organization's most important business function: serving its customers.[4]

---

[3] Since organizations often hire former police officers whom have very little actual security experience to manage their security function, it's not unusual that they would "use what they know."

[4] Although there's no perfect customer service-oriented conflict resolution system, attempts to resolve conflict must involve a broad understanding of basic business principles.

GETTING THE BALANCE RIGHT

There are also great distinctions in the *manner* of interpersonal contact between public police officers and private security personnel. Security personnel approach (or should approach) subject interaction the way business stakeholders do, placing a high value on customer service, such as *accommodation* and *negotiation*. Unlike private security personnel, police officers tend to approach subject interaction with much less concern for individual needs and a greater focus on the generalized needs of the community. In contrast to the law enforcement community, the private market thrives on *customer service* and positive customer feedback.[5]

It's unfortunate that public law enforcement community safety philosophies have crept into the private security industry and into private organizations, since they exacerbate the challenges of resolving conflict, protecting people, and maintaining safe organizations.

Unlike private organizations, police departments don't have a profit motive, nor do they have to compete for market share the way private organizations do. Although police departments need to be responsive to community needs, they don't lose market share as private organizations do if their community is offended by their conflict resolution strategies. (In fact, offending the right community members, the criminals, may be a useful public community safety tactic.) However, in the private market, if the community resists an organization's conflict resolution strategies, they may respond by taking their business elsewhere! In today's very competitive marketplace, organizational safety programs that don't consider the consumer's needs are, in effect, failures!

Useful Methods and Models

Although both police officers and private security personnel are responsible for maintaining safe communities, they use different safety models[6] and resources to achieve their goals. Police officers use *enforcement* as the primary method for creating safe communities; private security personnel use (or should use) *advisement* and *protection* as their primary methods.

Besides these underlying differences, these two industries also use distinctive conflict resolution resources to accomplish their safety goals. Unlike private

---

[5] Once an individual's resistance escalates beyond simple passive aggressiveness, they're no longer a "customer." Although a reliable conflict resolution system needs to account for a variety of inappropriate customer behaviors, there also needs to be a clear line that, when crossed, invalidates the subject's customer status and reclassifies the individual as a noncustomer—that is, a trespasser.

[6] Organizational safety models are detailed in Chapter 3.

security personnel, the law enforcement community has myriad physical conflict resolution options and resources available only to them. These include helicopters, K9 units, mutual aid, special response teams, and various weapon options, to name a few. Unlike police officers, the vast majority of private security personnel don't even carry, nor do they have access to, defensive weapons.

BUSINESS-BASED CONFLICT RESOLUTION STRATEGIES

To effectively resolve conflict and maintain safe organizations, security personnel need access to a full spectrum of strategies, including the use of protective action. However, many organizations don't see a *business value* in using protective action to resolve conflict. Many organizations wholeheartedly acknowledge that *physical* strategies are necessary and appropriate for resolving conflict, but only if used by the police. Organizations simply don't believe it's worth the risk to allow their own employees to use physical force to resolve conflict.

As a security consultant, I've had hundreds of conversations with stakeholders who are sincerely convinced that any physical contact between security personnel and uncooperative subjects is never a good business decision. They argue it's always best to call the police and let them deal with uncooperative subjects rather than allow their own security personnel to get involved. However, when there's the potential for customers, employees, visitors, or others to be physically injured, it's never a good idea to wait for help to arrive, especially when security personnel are already on the scene.

INTEGRATING VARIOUS APPROACHES

Since security personnel play an important role in conflict resolution and organizational safety, their activities need to be integrated into businesses' broad organizational processes.

When security personnel understand basic business principles, they're more likely to apply protective action in a manner that supports their organization's primary business mission.

Since private organizations exist for vastly different reasons than public police departments, it's important that security personnel understand and act according to these respective differences. The main reason private organizations exist is to create profit and remain financially viable so that they can meet the needs of their customers and, if possible, increase their market share or influence. The success of private organizations depends on their ability to remain profitable, competitive, and socially relevant in their unique market. These private and public distinctions need to be reflected in an organization's approved conflict resolution strategies.

DEALING WITH STRUCTURAL IMPEDIMENTS

Often an organization's political and social hierarchy is a major impediment to organizational safety. Organizational sociopolitical power plays an important role in the conflict resolution process and in the success of many other community safety tasks. Since it's a difficult process to describe and explain and it draws unwanted attention to an often unexamined organizational weakness, sociopolitical power is rarely discussed. Many organizations assign the direct oversight of their security function to *another* nonsecurity stakeholder group (e.g., support services, human resources, accounting, operations, or facilities) that's organizationally situated low in the sociopolitical power structure, which naturally inhibits the security personnel's organizational influence. This political structure situates the senior security stakeholder, typically the security director or manager, several rungs down the corporate ladder compared to other departmental heads.[7] Unfortunately, this arrangement also positions the security *function,* and the corresponding conflict resolution *processes,* at the lowest levels of the organization's power structure.

To further exacerbate these sociopolitical dynamics, the security manager's nonsecurity direct report often has limited, if any, security expertise or experience.[8] *This arrangement creates additional impediments to developing cooperative stakeholder relationships and effective problem solving.*

Another weakness of this approach is that it forces the security manager's nonsecurity direct report to juggle two sets of organizational priorities and personal and sociopolitical agendas. Although it's true that some nonsecurity stakeholders may act based on their subordinates' expert advice, many others use these power inequities to their own organizational advantage. These additional layers of sociopolitical hierarchies and personal agendas interfere with timely critical decision making, decisive leadership, and effective conflict resolution, which in the end may *decrease* safety and *increase* potential civil or criminal liability.

Locating an organization's security function at the lowest sociopolitical levels limits personnel and mission effectiveness[9] and exacerbates unsafe conditions. Unfortunately, this *power-down* sociopolitical status is the norm in most organizations. When organizations fail to communicate—across *all* internal and external stakeholder

---

[7] A vice president of security once told me that even after he was promoted to VP status, he was still the least influential member of the senior staff. The creation of a VP position is an important step in the professionalization process, but there are still other sociopolitical obstacles to overcome to create higher levels of organizational relevance.

[8] Indeed.com listed an advertisement on May 7, 2012, seeking a director of facilities in Port Charlotte-Fawcett Memorial Hospital who would also be responsible for the organization's security function, but *no* security background is cited under "Qualifications"!

[9] See Chapter 10 for a more detailed exposition of social power and conflict resolution.

groups—the importance of cooperating with security personnel and the consequences for their failure,[10] these sociopolitical inequalities are reinforced. In fact, all too often security personnel are the only stakeholder group who are "fair game" to berate, mock, or bully, and sometimes it happens with *tacit* approval of senior stakeholders!

Tracy Wallach, who conducts research in Peace and Conflict studies, argues that these kinds of stakeholder attitudes may influence other stakeholders. Although Wallach is not writing about security personnel, her conclusions are relative to the formation of stakeholder attitudes. She writes, "In an organization, the process of a particular group within it tends to reflect the larger organizational culture, the assumptions, values, and beliefs associated with a particular business or profession, which is, in turn, influenced by the culture of the larger community and nation" (Wallach, p. 87). These underlying organizational *cultural* attitudes (whether they're deliberate or inadvertent) create uncooperative attitudes that influence relationships between security personnel and community members.

These organizational structures may also create impressions among other stakeholders that the security *task* and the security *personnel* have a lower *value* than do other organizational tasks or personnel. In some organizations, this social dynamic has created an environment in which almost *any* other stakeholder feels justified in "telling security what to do"![11] Where a particular business function is socially and politically situated within an organization's hierarchy impacts its effectiveness and also communicates its *value* (or a lack thereof) to organizational stakeholders. Security personnel often *perceive* this organizational positioning as a lack of value that influences the often-heard complaint of "not being appreciated." The truth is, powerless stakeholders are unable to effectively resolve conflict and maintain safe communities.

These sociopolitical hierarchies also influence security training. Since members of the security department has to rely on other nonsecurity stakeholders to articulate their needs, including the need for training and funding, other sociopolitical and personal agendas may take priority over their needs. There may be "political" barriers that make it difficult for nonsecurity stakeholders to communicate the importance of security personnel training up their chain of command.

Summary

Effective organizational safety principles need to both "protect and serve" a business's interests. Integrating conflict resolution strategies into an organization's

---

[10] The failure to communicate this organizational safety imperative may be directly related to the absence of senior security managers sitting at the "organizational table of influence."

[11] This unfortunate dynamic is further complicated when the security function is "contracted out" and security personnel are not thought of as part of the organization.

basic operating principles is important for maintaining safe and secure organizations. The strategies businesses use to create and maintain organizational safety and resolve conflict need to be *natural* extensions of their underlying business philosophy.

RECOMMENDATIONS

1. Integrate organizational safety with business operating principles.
2. Reposition/move the organization's security function higher up in the organization's sociopolitical hierarchy.
3. De-emphasize or replace public law enforcement community safety principles and philosophies with business-focused conflict resolution strategies.

Reference

Security Law Newsletter. Student files $5 million lawsuit against college after campus rape. Strafford Publications. Saunders, V. Sw., 2012. Or. Cmty. Coll., No.11-06391 (D. Or. Complaint filed 12/2/2011), January 2012; Web: <media.straffordpub.com/products/security-law-newsletter/free-sample.pdf> 31.05.12.

Chapter 3

Employing Organizational Safety Models

The Problem

Organizations currently use ineffective and counterproductive organizational safety models.

Introduction

To successfully resolve conflict, organizations need to use an organizational safety model that maximizes safety and supports organizations' primary business functions. The most popular approaches to organizational safety used by most private organizations are philosophically based on:

1. Enforcement
2. Observing and reporting
3. Protection

Although there are other approaches to organizational safety models, most of them incorporate some aspects of these foundational ideas. Unfortunately, enforcement- and observe-and-report-based organizational safety models don't provide

21

the highest levels of organizational safety. Observe-and-report models don't provide physical protection; enforcement models often exacerbate interpersonal field conflict.

Process

Unlike observe-and-report and enforcement organizational safety models, the lesser-used *observe, report, advise, and protect* (ORAP) model maximizes organizational safety by providing high levels of physical and liability protections and doesn't interfere with an organization's primary business mission.

The Observe-and-Report Model

Unfortunately, observe-and-report organizational safety models have become the current national security industry standard. In fact, this model is recommended by most state security licensing agencies. In California the Bureau of Security and Investigative Services (BSIS), the state agency that licenses private security guards, promotes this model.[1] Unfortunately, some organizations believe the observe-and-report model is the best organizational safety model available to organizations. (This is another example of the many unexamined assumptions that continue to persist in the security industry![2]). It's true that this model minimizes liability associated with inappropriate security personnel force. However, liability associated with the use of *inappropriate force* is much less than the *total* liabilities related to security personnel inaction!

The observe-and-report model has become embedded in the industry for two reasons. First, many state security guard licensing bureaus advocate for these types of behavioral limits primarily based on safety concerns, not on efficiency or effectiveness. Since most basic security personnel[3] are hired with little or no experience, receive just the basic levels of state-mandated training, are low paid, often work

---

[1] In California, the BSIS publishes the *Powers to Arrest Manual* (p. 22). Unfortunately, some consider these observe-and-report suggested personnel behavioral boundaries as legal mandates. These guidelines do not forbid security personnel from intervening, nor is intervention a violation of their standard.

[2] Most state security guard regulatory rules are created and administered by former police officers. Oddly, many, if not the majority, of these former law enforcement personnel "rule makers" have never worked as security guards!

[3] Professional security personnel are individuals who work directly for an organization's own security department (proprietary), who work in teams (they don't normally work alone), and who are hired, trained, supervised, and held accountable to high organizational, departmental, and professional standards.

alone, and are rarely closely supervised, the risk to both the security individual and the organization is naturally high if these types of security personnel were to become physically involved with uncooperative subjects.

Another reason this "hands-off" organizational safety model remains popular is that it is supported by a majority of senior nonsecurity organizational stakeholders who sponsor and fund security operations. A noncontact approach to conflict resolution is a philosophical fit for many stakeholders who have concluded (I would argue, uncritically and primarily anecdotally) that security personnel create more problems than they solve when they become physically engaged with uncooperative subjects. The prevailing wisdom among many professional risk managers posits that when security personnel become physically engaged with subjects, the risk elevates to unacceptable levels. This risk/benefit assessment may be accurate for basic security personnel but not for professional security personnel.[4]

The obvious weakness of an observe-and-report organizational safety model is that it prohibits security personnel from intervening to physically protect victims of violence. However, proponents of this noncontact model argue that even though personnel are prohibited from intervening, their visual presence provides value by deterring criminal activity. This deterrence philosophy contends that criminal activity is minimized because potential criminals see uniformed security personnel and are then deterred from engaging in criminal activity. However, when crime prevention through "visual deterrence" fails,[5] security personnel are prohibited from intervening; they can only report violations or criminal activity to other responsible stakeholders, such as supervisors or the police. Security personnel operating under an observe-and-report organizational safety model are the "eyes and ears," not the hands, of the community.

▌ The Enforcement Model

Some corporations use enforcement (or quasi-enforcement) organizational safety models, or their preferred organizational safety approaches incorporate high levels of enforcement. Although enforcement may be an effective strategy in some contexts and for some stakeholder groups, it is not usually an effective conflict

---

[4]These organizational risks are not unique to security personnel. Pick any departmental personnel and allow them to work alone; pay them minimum wage; don't require prior industry experience; don't supervise them; don't hold them accountable to high organizational, departmental, or professional standards, and then require them to solve complicated interpersonal problems. The results would be the same!

[5]Uniformed security personnel may deter property crimes, but there's very little evidence that visual deterrence alone will constrain violent individuals from physically harming others.

resolution strategy when used by private security personnel. In a private context, enforcement activities often exacerbate interpersonal tensions. These artificially *created* tensions decrease personnel safety and create distractions from an organization's core organizational safety mission.

Unlike security personnel, police officers use enforcement as an effective conflict resolution strategy for creating and maintaining safe public communities. However, unlike police officers, private security personnel don't possess the enabling statutory authority and extensive officer training that empower its effectiveness. Since private security personnel don't have the requisite enabling attributes to resolve conflict through enforcement activities, it's rarely a good idea for private security personnel to be involved in enforcement activities.[6]

Adversarial Techniques

Involving private security personnel in enforcement activities creates adversarial relationships with community members. Enforcement activities interfere with security personnel developing cooperative partnerships with other organizational stakeholders. When organizational members perceive security personnel as *partners*, they're more likely to become willing participants in an organization's corporate community safety mission.

Another concern with involving security personnel in enforcement activities is the potential for their mere presence to create hostility. Community members don't like being hassled, especially by uniformed security personnel who often focus their attention on bad behavior. When community members perceive security personnel as peacemakers, it's much easier to manage and resolve conflict. When security personnel are involved in enforcement or quasi-enforcement activities, their interactions are naturally perceived as adversarial. When security personnel operate in enforcement mode, there's always the possibility that interpersonal field conflict may escalate and become violent.

When security personnel operate in enforcement mode, the potential of creating a hostile environment increases.

The death of Kelly Thomas may be a representative example of the weakness of enforcement mode. In July 2011, a violent field conflict occurred in the city of Fullerton, California, between Fullerton police officers and Kelly Thomas. After a physical altercation with the police, Thomas died. This field conflict led to the death of a young man and the arrest of two police officers for murder!

---

[6]One exception may be using security personnel for parking enforcement activities. However, creating separate and distinct parking enforcement personnel (or a division) will decrease potential interpersonal field conflicts.

Tony Rackauckas, the Orange County, California, District Attorney, pushed to prosecute the involved police officers for murder based on an allegation that the officers "created the environment" that led to Thomas's death. At a press conference on September 21, 2011, Rackauckas stated, "The biggest shame about this case is the fact that it could have been avoided."[7] Rackauckas went on to say, "[Fullerton police officer] Ramos set in motion the events that led to the death of Kelly Thomas ..." (Orange County, California, District Attorney's Office).

This case highlights the new social reality for first-responder personnel. More communities are now thinking along these lines in assessing the outcomes of physical interactions between personnel and uncooperative subjects. The claim of "setting events into motion" could be made against any private security individual (or any uniformed authority figure), especially when they're involved in enforcement activities.[8] If organizations can't find other solutions for modifying unacceptable organizational behavior and resolving conflict and they require enforcement activities, they should find other internal or external stakeholders, not security personnel, to these process violations. We are not proposing that organizations abdicate all enforcement activities; enforcement is an important and necessary operational task for successful organizations. However, when security personnel become involved in enforcement (or quasi-enforcement) activities, there's a greater chance that these interactions will escalate to violence.

Paradoxically, security personnel often end up being assigned enforcement duties because they argued for it or because they didn't forcefully resist it being assigned to them. Since there are abundant opportunities in every community to apply enforcement techniques, security departments assume that it's a simple way to create relevance or to increase or maintain their operating budgets. (To a lesser extent, some stakeholders may think security enforcement activities actually create safer communities.) Additionally, because of an overrepresentation of police-oriented security personnel in the security industry, enforcement activities naturally seem like an effective strategy. Over time these self-assigned (or unresisted) enforcement duties have become embedded in organizational culture (and codified in policy), and now community members *expect* security personnel to enforce certain rules, policies, or laws.

This approach to creating relevance often backfires, since corporate enforcement activities don't always improve organizational safety. In fact, these activities often lead to *increases* in community tensions and a *greater potential* for conflict

---

[7] The DA's focus was on what actions the officers could have avoided at the exclusion of Thomas's. Logically, actions taken by all involved parties would need to be taken into consideration to make a rational conclusion. However, there's an important lesson contained in the DA's statements.

[8] To combat these allegations, personnel should be trained in verbal tactics and verbal de-escalation. See Chapter 10 for a more detailed exposition of these tactics.

to escalate to violence.[9] Often, senior stakeholders assign their security department enforcement duties without fully understanding the unintended consequences of involving private security personnel in those duties.

The key to successful conflict resolution *through enforcement* is assigning the right enforcement stakeholder group to the corresponding type of conflict that enforcement is best equipped to resolve. Calling the police to ticket or tow an unlawfully parked vehicle, or a dean of students suspending a dangerous student, are effective forms of enforcement-based conflict resolution. These enforcement examples are nonsecurity-related methods for resolving conflict. However, in both of these examples, if the violators became aggressive, security personnel could be utilized as peacekeepers, a mission-focused task, whereas other stakeholders would function as the "enforcers."

The Observe, Report, Advise, and Protect Model

The observe, report, advise, and protect (ORAP) organizational safety model is the most effective conflict resolution model available to organizations that employ security personnel. The ORAP model allows an organization to "serve and protect" its human and business interests; it protects people, property, reputations, and an organization's ability to financially compete in its unique market. Unlike other organizational safety models, the ORAP model empowers stakeholder synergy to aid in the effective and efficient management of conflict and is easily integrated into an organization's basic business operating principles.

The primary reason the ORAP model is the most effective conflict resolution system is that it accounts for the *natural* limitations of every stakeholder group, including security personnel, while maximizing individual stakeholder expertise in making *positive* contributions to the conflict resolution process.

The ORAP organizational safety model establishes clear *role and responsibility* distinctions for all stakeholders, including security and police personnel, who have the primary responsibility for organizational safety. The two most important functions of the ORAP model are *advisement* and *protection.*

The advisory function is one of the most important and overlooked roles of an effective conflict resolution system. When security personnel operate in an *advisory* role, they identify potential interpersonal field conflict and physical safety hazards. Physical safety hazards, like trip hazards, can be reported to the proper stakeholder group for correction, whereas individual safety violations, such as

---

[9] See Chapter 4 for a more detailed exposition of one of the social-psychological processes that create a propensity for security personnel to use physical conflict resolution strategies (Security Attire Identity Dissonance, or SAID).

threats of violence, are confronted and the involved individuals are advised to correct their behavior. This *proactive* approach to conflict resolution often keeps minor safety concerns from escalating to major problems. In this role, security personnel advise potential safety violators of their inappropriate behavior and advise them of the consequences of their failure to correct it. Since private security personnel have virtually no authority and very little power to resolve conflict by themselves, their primary role in the conflict resolution process should be *advising* potential conflict makers to correct their inappropriate behavior.

When utilizing an ORAP organizational safety model, security personnel don't use physical action on nonviolent resistors to correct their inappropriate behavior.

The second, and perhaps the most important, benefit of the ORAP organizational safety model is physical *protection*. If an organizational safety violator's behavior has the potential to lead to *immediate* physical harm or if it creates *active* physical harm, security personnel are authorized to physically intervene to protect individuals. We believe professional security personnel are obligated (or they should be obligated) as a condition of employment (or as a condition of continued employment) to physically protect from *unarmed* physical attacks[10] individuals who are at risk of being physically injured. However controversial this position may be, it's a reasonable expectation that trained professional security personnel ought to be required to provide a tangible and quantifiable value to their organizations, such as protecting people from injury.

Failure to physically protect community members should be considered both a moral and a legal failing of responsible organizations. Observe-and-report organizational models don't support these obligations.

Empowered Stakeholders

The ORAP organizational safety model enables each stakeholder's unique power, authority, and training to maximize their conflict resolution potential. Many organizational safety problems are easily resolved by simply advising the involved individual of their inappropriate behavior. Some types of conflict are better resolved by internal stakeholders, whereas other types need to be resolved by external stakeholders.

Interpersonal Field Conflict Dynamics

The ORAP organizational safety model provides personnel with efficient assessment tools and a reliable conflict resolution process that maximizes individual

---

[10] Security personnel should never confront armed subjects unless they too are armed.

stakeholder authority, power, and expertise. An efficient assessment of the *interpersonal field conflict dynamics* operating at the time of each unique interaction is a key to successful conflict resolution. During field conflict, security personnel are often the first individuals to make contact with the involved parties.

Security personnel first responders need to assess the unique interpersonal field conflict dynamics in play at the time of the interaction. They're responsible for assessing it and acquiring information that's necessary for facilitating successful conflict resolution. The following information is necessary for a reliable interpersonal field conflict dynamics assessment:

1. Is there active physical harm in progress or a *potential* for immediate physical harm?
2. Is the violator affiliated or nonaffiliated with the organization?
3. What is the specific organizational safety violation?
4. What is the subject's contact stage?
5. What is the subject's behavioral phase?

Once security personnel become involved in a field conflict, the most important consideration is restoring or creating a safe environment for all involved parties. An interpersonal field conflict dynamics assessment plays an important role in successful conflict resolution.

Affiliation is determined by the type of relationship that exists between the organization and the organizational safety violator. *Affiliated* subjects (such as patients, family members, visitors, students, faculty, staff, vendors, or customers) have a direct relationship to the organization, whereas *nonaffiliated* individuals (such as criminal trespassers) are those who have an indirect relationship with the organization. Technically, any time a subject is involved in a conflict that takes place on an organization's property, the organization has a *de facto* relationship with the subject. However, affiliated relationships create higher levels of accountability, responsibility, and responses than do nonaffiliated relationships.

Organizational safety violations are the laws, rules, policies, or procedures that are violated.

The subject *contact stage* is either initial or secondary. Sometimes security personnel are the first (or initial) stakeholders to confront inappropriate behavior; at other times they're called in after (or secondarily to) personnel have already been interacting with the subject.

The *behavioral phase* is determined by the subject's emotional state at the time of the interaction. The three behavioral phases are passive aggressive, direct aggressive, and violent.

Passive-aggressive individuals are characterized by initial verbal uncooperativeness and verbally abusive and physically noncompliant behavior, but they are *not* physically assaultive. Verbal conflict resolution techniques are *usually* effective with passive-aggressive individuals.

Directly aggressive individuals are characterized by directed and emotionally intense verbal and physical aggressiveness and threats of violence, but their behavior is not actually assaultive. Directly aggressive individuals present a conflict resolution dilemma because, under some conditions, verbal conflict resolution techniques *may* be effective, whereas under other conditions a subject's emotional state will continue to escalate and physical strategies are needed.

Violent individuals have either exhibited assaultive behavior or are an immediate physical threat. At this behavioral phase, verbal conflict resolution strategies are inappropriate. Assaultive behavior *cannot* be managed or resolved with verbal strategies; physical intervention is necessary![11]

Resolution Misalignment

Conflict resolution involves interacting with many different conflict scenarios, various violator relationships, complicated interpersonal dynamics, and numerous organizational safety violations. One of the keys to successful conflict resolution is assigning the stakeholder group that is best equipped to manage and resolve the *unique* conflict scenario. To facilitate efficient conflict resolution, organizations should create a conflict resolution matrix that includes a comprehensive list of stakeholders correlated to the various conflict resolution variables.

Unfortunately, organizations often assign the *wrong* stakeholder group to process interpersonal field conflict, which escalates tensions, decreases safety, and creates unnecessary potential liability. Stakeholders should not get involved in areas they're not adequately trained for and equipped to deal with. Conversely, trained and equipped problem solvers need to act proactively by asserting themselves into conflict scenarios they're prepared to safely resolve.

The two most common *conflict resolution* failures occur when security personnel try to manage highly volatile conflict (e.g., armed individuals) themselves instead of calling the police, or conversely, when security personnel call the police to help them when they *could have* resolved the conflict themselves.

Conflict resolution misalignment decreases organizational safety and wastes the time, energy, and resources of other busy stakeholders (e.g., corporate administrators or the police).[12]

---

[11] "Verbal-only" conflict resolution systems such as MOAB are ineffective when dealing with assaultive behavior because once a subject becomes a physical threat, that person's behavior can no longer be managed; it has to be stopped.

[12] Successful organizations need to establish beneficial working partnerships with all stakeholder groups, including the police, and be aware that wasting their time and resources is not a good business decision.

Organizational Safety Associates

Another important change associated with the implementation of an ORAP organizational safety model is a personnel title name change. A change from *security officer* to *organizational safety associate* (OSA) is both a philosophical and a pragmatic change; it helps modify quasi-military/law enforcement perceptions of an organization's security personnel. For some organizations, implementing the organizational safety associate mode will be part of a complete paradigm change; for others it may be a minor adjustment to their current security officer model. These changes are more than just visual or semantic; they're principled changes that reinforce an organization's primary mission. (A change in verbiage is important because it supports and reinforces an organization's focus and eventually leads to a change in behavior.[13])

A change in personnel titles from military/law enforcement-based, such as *officer* or *sergeant*, to more business-oriented titles, such as *associate* or *manager*, align security personnel titles with the organization's other nonsecurity stakeholders. This change is important because it helps with security personnel integration and stakeholder cohesiveness.[14]

Organizational safety associates operating under an ORAP organizational safety model are authorized to use protective action to resolve interpersonal issues. We define *protective action* (used for protective interventions) as follows: physical subject contact, whether accomplished through personal body contact or with a protective device or tool made for the narrow purpose of protecting individuals (including security personnel, employees, customers, or others) from immediate or active physical harm, applied in a manner that minimizes injury while maximizing safety for all involved subjects.

Support Mode

When dealing with potential organizational safety violators and violations that don't involve the potential for active or immediate physical harm, security personnel function in *support mode* and have two *noncontact options*:

1. Advise the violator of their inappropriate behavior and request they correct it.[15]
2. If the violator fails to comply with the personnel request, they then attempt to identify the violator's affliction status and the specific organizational safety

---

[13] A personnel title change also supports the development of a unique private security "identity," as detailed in Chapter 4.

[14] A personnel title change also plays a positive role in minimizing the negative effects of security attire identity dissonance (SAID). See Chapter 4 for a more detailed exposition of SAID.

[15] Advising is one function of an ORAP organizational safety model.

violation so that they can determine whether they should process it themselves or assign it to another stakeholder who has the requisite power, authority, and training *and* is best equipped to process the violator or violation (e.g., Dean of Students, Human Resources, or the police, to name a few options).

When security personnel are processing nonphysical safety-related organizational safety violators or violations, their primary role is to support other stakeholders in the conflict resolution process.

For example, if an organization has a nonsmoking policy, and security personnel were to make initial contact with a subject who was smoking a cigarette, they would advise the smoker of the policy and ask for policy compliance. However, if the smoker refuses to cooperate, security personnel would contact *another* nonsecurity stakeholder to process the violation. Security personnel do *not* take enforcement action while operating in support mode.

Protective Mode

On the other hand, if security personnel interact with organizational safety violators that involve the potential for active or immediate physical harm, they have several contact options:

1. Determine whether the violator is an affiliated or nonaffiliated subject.
2. Physically intervene, if it's safe and appropriate to do so. (Step 1 and Step 2 could be interchanged for safety purposes.)
3. Apply the protective action option that's appropriate to the violator's affiliation status, community standard violation, and subject's resistance level,[16] as authorized by the organization's policy.
4. Contact additional responsible stakeholders as needed for support and processing (e.g., police, paramedics, or dean of students).

When security personnel are processing physical safety-related organizational safety violations, they operate in *protective* mode.

As in the previous nonsmoking policy violation example, if an administrator were to advise a subject to stop smoking and the smoker became verbally abusive toward the administrator, it would be appropriate for security personnel to become involved—but only to keep the peace and ensure that the interaction doesn't escalate to violence. However, if the interaction did escalate, security personnel would step in to resolve it.

The ORAP organizational safety model is superior to other organizational safety models. First, it offers a systematic method for accessing potential negative conflict

---

[16] See Chapter 11 for a more detailed exposition of correlating subject resistance with protective action.

interaction. Next, personal protection for organizational and community members is prioritized. Third, if individuals are in physical danger, security personnel are authorized to intervene. Fourth, stakeholders get involved only when they have the requisite authority, power, expertise, and training to best manage and resolve the unique conflict dynamics. Finally, security personnel (organizational safety associates) are not assigned to enforcement tasks (or, if they are, they are limited in scope), allowing them to stay focused on their primary organizational safety mission: To protect and serve.

Summary

The ORAP organizational safety model is the best model for maintaining safe communities. To successfully resolve interpersonal field conflict and maintain safe organizations, organizations need to use the most effective organizational safety model available. An organization's security personnel, including other internal and external stakeholder groups, should use their unique authority, power, expertise, and training to support an organization's ability to safely resolve conflict and remain financially viable, competitive, and socially relevant in their unique market.

RECOMMENDATIONS

1. Implement the ORAP organizational safety model.
2. Change security personnel titles from law enforcement/military-based to organizational-based titles.
3. Clearly articulate each stakeholder's role and responsibilities in the conflict resolution process.
4. Maximize conflict resolution efficiency by establishing a conflict resolution matrix for all stakeholders.

Reference

Rackauckas, T., 2011. Remarks by district attorney Tony Rackauckas investigation results and filing decision regarding the death of Kelly Thomas. 21 September 2011; Web: Office of the District Attorney, Orange County CA, < www.orangecountyda.com > 21.09.11.

Chapter 4

Presenting a Professional Image

The Problem

The private security industry and organizations that employ security personnel have failed to create a unique, distinct, and effective identity.

Introduction

Private security personnel have a personality disorder; they're not sure who they want to be! At times they want to be associated with the law enforcement industry; at other times, with the private security industry. The lack of a consistent and stable identity creates many challenges for the security industry and its security personnel, including low wages, inconsistent working conditions, and a lack of organizational influence. However, perhaps the greatest problem associated with a failure to create a reliable security identity is its impact on conflict resolution.

The security officer's uniform or attire plays an important role in impression management, identity formation, and conflict resolution. Unfortunately, many organizations have overlooked how something as basic as a uniform can help or hinder

33

conflict resolution. Organizations make the mistake of allowing their security personnel to wear uniforms that create impressions that their security personnel are police officers. Public impressions created by uniform choices impact both internal and external customers and can impact conflict resolution. When employees perceive their organizations' security personnel as "enforcement" officers and not community partners, barriers to cooperation are created. Similarly, when customers and visitors perceive security personnel as police officers, unreasonable expectations of service are created. A distinctive "nonenforcement" security uniform plays an important role in developing cooperative partnerships with both internal and external customers, conflict resolution, and organizational safety.

Process

Organizational members don't want to be policed at work, but they *do* expect organizations to maintain safe environments without creating a "police state." If security personnel are perceived as *police-like* because of their uniforms, duty gear, and personal demeanor, organizational members may unconsciously project negative and uncooperative public policing attitudes onto private security personnel, making it more difficult for them to manage and resolve interpersonal field conflict.

Uniforms and Duty Gear

Selecting the right color, type, or style of security uniform and duty equipment that private security personnel carry plays an important role in creating an effective security identity that facilitates conflict resolution. Simply put, the uniform that an employee wears is a statement of an organization's purpose. Private organizations typically create mission statements that focus on the *protection of people and property,* so their security personnel's uniform should reflect that mission. Since the vast majority of organizations that employ security personnel don't (or shouldn't) enforce laws, rules, or policies, law enforcement and military-type uniforms and duty equipment may be *counterproductive* to an organization's published mission.

The selection of uniforms and duty equipment should be the result of a thorough security task assessment, integrated with a detailed risk and vulnerability assessment of personnel and organizational safety. Unfortunately, many security departments make seemingly pragmatic but counterproductive and unwise uniform choices that purposefully mimic the law enforcement community. Some falsely argue that wearing police-type uniforms creates "perceptions of authority" that aid in the conflict resolution process. This belief is another unexamined and untested community safety assumption carried over from the law enforcement industry.

Uniform Attributes

The color or type of uniform worn by an individual is *not* the primary reason for public perceptions of authority. Although many security stakeholders argue that wearing police-colored and police-style uniforms *creates* authority, they make the mistake of confusing *uniform* attributes with *personal* attributes. How an individual wears a uniform, or that person's personal attributes (e.g., height, body type, physical fitness level, age, or demeanor), play a much bigger role in the creation of public perceptions of authority than do uniform attributes (e.g., color, color combinations, fabric, or style). Since most police officers have *positive* personal attributes *and* high levels of authority, it's easy to conflate uniform and personal attributes and falsely conclude that the *uniform* is responsible for perceptions of authority. Unlike police officers, private security personnel are generally not perceived by the public as having positive personal attributes.[1]

Another flaw in the belief that certain police-colored uniforms (e.g., dark navy blue shirts and pants) create authority is disproved by surveying the various uniform colors and styles worn by the global law enforcement community. Shirt and pants colors and combinations range among white, light blue, green, khaki, dark blue, tan, brown, black, and yellow. Similarly, uniform styles range from causal to military based. Since police officers throughout the United States wear various colors and types of uniforms, its seems implausible that a specific color or uniform style would be responsible for creating universal perceptions of authority.

Authority is created primarily through statutory codes and secondarily through personal attributes and social processes. Unlike police officers, private security personal authority is created primarily through personal attributes and secondarily by the behavioral boundaries developed by property owners.

"You are What You Wear!"

Everyone—not just uniformed personnel—is a poser. Not much has changed since Shakespeare said "All the world's a stage." What one wears is part of the *public pose* of creating and managing public impressions. All professions, from the UPS driver to an airline pilot, use *attire, manner, and setting* to create specific public impressions that set themselves apart from other people and other professions. It's

---

[1]Failure to create serious physical fitness standards, like the ones police departments have established, is responsible for the high percentage of obviously unfit or obese security personnel that are responsible for creating universal and stable negative perceptions of private security personnel.

obvious that there's a social-psychological relationship between the way a person *dresses*, the way the wearer is *perceived* by others, the way the wearer *processes* those impressions, and the way the wearer *acts*. The right security uniform should create and maintain a unique security *identify* that helps, not hinders, the conflict resolution process.

Everyone has experienced the feeling of acting like how they felt because of what they were wearing, whether it's because of a suit that fits just right or a feeling that's created when we're getting dressed for a special event. There's an abundance of scientific research in the area of clothing, perceptions, and behavior. Drs. Adam Galinsky and Hajo Adam of Northwestern University have recently extended a new area of clothing research and are credited with coining the term enclothed cognition. The theory suggests that we think with both our brains and our bodies. What one wears creates perceptions of the wearer, and in turn these perceptions affect the wearer's behavior. Prior to this new research, little attention was paid to the social-psychological processes that activate the wearer's behavior based on the wearer's interpretations of how others perceived the wearer. The researchers note, "The current research provides initial support for the enclothed cognition perspective that clothes can have profound and systematic psychological and behavior consequence of the wearer." The researchers go on to say, "… the effects of wearing a piece of clothing cannot be reduced to the wearer simply feeling identified with the clothing. Instead, there seems to be something special about the physical experience of wearing a piece of clothing, and this experience constitutes a critical component of enclothed cognition" (Adam and Galinsky, 2012 p. 5).

The socio-psychological connection between attire and behavior is well established. In fact, it's not limited to the UPS driver, the airline pilot, or the security officer. This socio-psychological process is similar to the process that affects the way trick-or-treating children feel and act when they dress up like Batman.

All organizations use attire as a pose or a way to create certain public impressions of their employees and their organization. Some organizations or industries prefer professional business attire, such as suits and dresses; others prefer a distinctive uniform. Doctors wear white jackets, nurses wear scrubs, college professors wear sports jackets with elbow patches. These clothing choices are often made to visually distinguish an organization's employees from one another, to distinguish employees from their competition, or to create a professional image. However, when private security personnel pose like they're police officers, they add an undesirable dimension—deception—to the legitimate reasons for wearing a distinctive uniform. Unfortunately, this kind of uniform deception has the potential to backfire, since the public doesn't like being tricked. Attempting to gain the cooperation of community members by manipulating them into believing that private security personnel have police power or authority they don't actually possess interferes with community partnerships and conflict resolution.

◼ SAID: Security Attire Identity Dissonance

Through our research and experience with private security personnel and the security industry, we've noticed a unique social-psychological relationship between the *type* of security uniform personnel wear and the way personnel act while wearing it. We've tentatively identified the social-psychological processes that are activated when security individuals wear police-type uniforms as *security attire identity dissonance,* or SAID.[2] SAID is activated when nonsworn, private security personnel wear police-type uniforms, carry police-type duty gear, and create feelings of authority and social power they don't actually possess.[3] Additionally, since the security industry is overrepresented by police-oriented individuals,[4] wearing police-type uniforms tends to create the familiar feelings of "being a police officer," which amplifies the effects of SAID.

Even though uniformed private security personnel intellectually know they're not police officers when they dress like them and interact with other police trappings such as police gear, police radios, and police codes, security personnel often find themselves in a constant state of emotional-psychological dissonance. In fact, cognitive dissonance theory suggests that all humans have a real physical need to resolve their psychological discomfort (Festinger, 1957 p. 20). According to the theory, all it takes to resolve cognitive dissonance is to act the way one feels.

Unfortunately, the emotional-psychological tension created when private security personnel wear police-type uniforms may create security personnel behavior that both relieves individuals' tension and creates interpersonal tension, which leads to decreases in security personnel safety and increases in potential criminal and civil liability.

Private security personnel often relieve their dissonance by acting in ways that make them feel like police officers. One way to relieve this tension is to deliberately (or subconsciously) insert oneself into intense field conflict situations that necessitate the use of authority, power, or physical force to resolve. Since private security personnel don't typically have the training, statutory authority, or social power to safely resolve conflicts by asserting authority, these "dissonance-relieving" behaviors often create or exacerbate interpersonal tension.

Our tentative findings indicate that when private security personnel wear distinctive "nonenforcement" uniforms,[5] they experience lower levels of

---

[2]This hypothesis was developed after years of surveying security personnel attitudes and through interviews with security personnel.

[3]The use of police/military-based personnel titles and the wearing of police-type uniforms work together to exacerbate the affects of SAID.

[4]See Chapter 8 for a more detailed exposition of police-oriented personnel.

[5]These uniforms have shirt-and-pants combinations, styles, and colors that make it obvious that security personnel are not police officers.

emotional-psychological dissonance than those who wear "police-type" uniforms. Lower levels of dissonance may minimize security personnel's use of inappropriate, inadequate, or excessive physical force, thus reducing potential civil and criminal liabilities and improving conflict resolution.

Presenting a False Image

Security personnel often waste their valuable and limited resources trying to manipulate community members into thinking they have authority and power they don't possess. Unfortunately, some private security departments *deliberately* adopt a "police-type" uniform with the stated (or implied) purpose of attempting to create the public impression that their security personnel have police power. These security personnel wear uniforms that are *identical* to public police agencies, and they carry similar protective or defensive tools or weapons. Some believe this incidental deception creates added protections, such as perceptions of authority that deter criminal behavior. Some argue that criminals may be dissuaded from assaulting security personnel if suspects are initially convinced that the security individual is a police officer. Unfortunately, this theory cuts both ways. Criminals are known to assault police officers simply based on being easily identified by their police uniforms! We don't think criminals who target cops will be dissuaded by the fact that security personnel are not actually police officers.

In the private market, security personnel authority is determined by the property owner (security personnel are agents of the owner or the responsible party) and secondarily through various statutory and regulatory requirements. Organizations create authority through written policies and socially through practical demonstrations of their organizational safety mission. However, organizations don't typically allow security personnel to operate at their full limits; they draw narrower behavioral boundaries in an attempt to protect their organization from certain liabilities.[6] Security personnel often use these restrictive behavioral limits and the organization's lack of social, political, or organizational support to justify their own creative attempts to manufacture authority. Although security personnel don't have power to create authority themselves, their individual and collective behavior does influence the way the community perceives them; positive perceptions of security personnel do create social influence.[7] To be clear, legitimate authority is not created by wearing police-type uniforms or by carrying certain kinds of equipment.

Since authority and social power play an important role in resolving conflict and creating safe environments, it's understandable that security personnel would want

---

[6] See Chapter 7 for a more detailed exposition of liability.
[7] See Chapter 10 for a more detailed exposition of social power.

high levels of authority for interacting with uncooperative, dangerous, or violent individuals. In an attempt to get what many legal statutes and organizations withhold, private security personnel often get creative by using deception in an attempt to create authority. The deliberate withholding of organizational authority influences personnel to act in various ways, including wearing police-type uniforms, carrying police-type gear, or acting like police officers, in an attempt to usurp organizational constraints and improve officer safety. Unfortunately, these activities often create the exact opposite effect: They further alienate community members and create additional barriers for positive community interactions. These barriers include:

1. Unrealistic community expectations
2. Psychological projection
3. Dysfunctional social groupings
4. Public perceptions of impersonating police officers

When security personnel dress like police officers, it elevates the community's expectations of service. Paradoxically, organizations also become dissatisfied with security personnel when they act like police officers in a *bad way* and when they *don't* act like police officers in a *good way*! Unlike security personnel, police officers have a wide array of resources and training to help support their communities' safety needs. Dressing like police officers creates an expectation that uniformed security personnel should be able to perform many of the same community safety tasks as police officers, including coming to a community member's aid under very complicated and potentially dangerous circumstances. This is especially problematic for organizations that allow their security personnel to dress like police officers while simultaneously prohibiting physical contact with uncooperative subjects.

There's a natural relationship between perceived expectations of service and actual service. From the community's perspective, not providing the same level of service as police officers, ("Especially since you look like them ...") may be perceived by the community as a cruel joke. The failure to meet the community members' expectations of service, especially after tricking them, creates negative community attitudes and leads to a lack of cooperation.

Another consequence of security personnel dressing like police officers is the likelihood that community members will project their own negative feelings and attitudes about police officers onto their private security personnel. The public often perceive police officers as aggressive and rude. Even law-abiding citizens develop negative attitudes toward police officers because of negative interpersonal experiences, such as getting a speeding ticket. In the context of creating safe public communities, these interpersonal behaviors may create some benefit for police officers, but in the private security market they're counterproductive. In the free market, there's an expectation of customer service that's characterized by being highly flexible, cooperative, and highly positively interpersonal.[8] Negative perceptions of an organization's "police personnel" create uncooperative community attitudes that ultimately interfere (consciously or unconsciously) with an organization's safety mission.

Another consequence of security personnel being perceived as police officers is the unintended consequence of creating an "us versus them" social dynamic. When security personnel are socially isolated from the community members they serve, it creates an impediment to the free flow of information and decreases personnel safety. When private security personnel dress (and sometimes act) like police officers, especially when personnel are involved in enforcement activities, community members may perceive them as spoil sports, or worse, fascists! Feelings of distrust may lead to increases in conflict and greater opportunity for simple conflict to escalate to violence.

When security personnel are perceived as part of "them," community members are less likely to provide strategic information that is necessary for resolving interpersonal field conflict and maintaining safe communities. Information is an important and necessary commodity for formulating proactive organizational safety strategies. Security personnel need to be perceived by community members as being part of "us" in order to maintain open lines of communication with the community members.

Physical and social protection from outsiders is one of the many benefits of being perceived by the community as a member of an *in-group* (Tajfel and Turner, 1992 p. 126). When security personnel are isolated from community members, they become "them." If security personnel become involved in a physical altercation and they're perceived as a member of the *out-group*, it may create an unwillingness for community members to come to their aid or to socially defend their actions after a critical field interaction. Although most communities have unsophisticated ways of defining in-groups and out-groups, police officers (and other authority figures) are generally not thought of as members of the in-group, especially if they're responsible for enforcing policies, rules, or laws.

However, when security personnel are socially integrated into the broad organizational stakeholder community, they're more likely to be considered part of the in-group, and community members are more likely to physically and philosophically defend them from outsiders.

Impersonating a Police Officer

Besides the pragmatic reasons for not allowing private security personnel to wear uniforms that look like those of police officers, there may also be legal considerations.

---

[8] Although there are great distinctions between sales-based customer service and safety-based customer service, private market organizations need to be sensitive to which types of conflict resolution strategies they utilize.

Most states have laws that specifically forbid nonsworn security officers from looking like or being confused with law enforcement officers. Although private security officers are required to wear a distinctive uniform, their uniform should not create public impressions that a security officer is a peace officer. In California, the Bureau of Security and Investigative Service (BSIS) and the California Business and Professions (B&P) Code forbid security officers from wearing a uniform "with the intent to give an impression that he/she is connected in any way with a government ... [law enforcement] agency ...."[9] California B&P Code section 7583.38 also states that local law enforcement agencies may regulate the wearing of a private security officer's uniform to make sure it's clearly distinguishable from their personnel. Additionally, most states make it a violation of law to impersonate a police officer.

Practically, even if wasn't a violation of the law to wear police-type uniforms, it's still a poor business decision to wear them. Police-type uniforms interfere with the projection of a professional security image because they create high levels of confusion among security personnel and the public. Allowing private security officers to wear police-type uniforms and carry police-type duty gear is a remnant of an age where enforcement[10] was thought to be the best way to resolve conflict and maintain safe organizations. However, since the primary mission of a security professional is to observe, report, advise, and protect, *not* enforce, the security individual's uniform should reflect this business-focused approach to conflict resolution.

Internal Challenges

Since police personnel and security personnel continually cross back and forth between these two vocations, there are strong personal ties between the law enforcement and security communities. Unfortunately, these relationships make it more difficult (and in some cases "politically" impossible) to openly discuss these and other related industry concerns. However, if the universal security industry is going to continue its professionalize process, it's important that they create a unique identity and develop a distinctive security uniform.[11]

Summary

Security personnel should not be perceived by community members as enforcers but rather as protectors—the *good guys*! Security personnel should be the

---

[9] California Business and Professions Code 7582.26.

[10] See Chapter 3 for a more detailed exposition of the various community safety models.

[11] See the uniform worn by Azusa Pacific University campus safety personnel in Azusa, California, as an excellent example.

stakeholder group that comes to the community's aid, 24/7/365, *not* the group that is perceived as "out to get" people. The truth is, it's difficult to be perceived as the good guys (part of the team) when security personnel dress and act like police officers and enforce policies, rules, or laws.

Something as simple as a uniform or a look has the power to create *impressions* about an organization's security personnel that ultimately help or hinder conflict resolution. Uniform and equipment selection is an important decision that many organizations and private security departments fail to take seriously. Selecting the right uniform and equipment that create a professional security identity plays an important role in conflict resolution, the development of community partnerships, and the creation of safe communities.

RECOMMENDATIONS

1. Choose uniform colors and uniform styles that make it *impossible* for the community to confuse security personnel with law enforcement personnel.
2. Carry only protective tools that are necessary for meeting the organization's *actual* organizational safety goals.
3. Maintain legitimate authority through nonuniform or duty gear-related social processes.

References

Adam, H., Galinsky, A.D., 2012. Enclothed cognition. J. Exp. Soc. Psychol. http://dx.doi.org/10.1016/j.jesp.2012.02.008 (in press).

Festinger, L.A., 1957. Theory of Cognitive Dissonance. Stanford University Press, Stanford, CA.

Tajfel, H., Turner, J.C., 1992. The social identity theory of intergroup behavior. In: Gudykunst, W.B., Kim, Y.Y. (Eds.), Readings on Communicating with Strangers McGraw-Hill, New York.

Chapter 5

Protecting Your Reputation

The Problem

Organizations are unable to effectively resolve conflict without damaging their public reputation.

Introduction

Managing the public's perception of an organizational safety program, including perceptions of its conflict resolution strategies and security personnel activities, plays an important role in conflict resolution, organizational safety, and reputation protection. Successful organizations typically do an effective job of creating positive public impressions of their products or services while simultaneously managing negatives ones. However, many of these same organizations fail to include organizational safety as a service for which public impressions also need to be managed.

One of the ways organizations succeed is by being competitive and socially relevant in their marketplace. Although physical conflict resolution strategies are **43** necessary for maintaining organizational safety and resolving interpersonal field conflict, their use has the *potential* to create negative perceptions of an organization, impacting their social relevance and damaging their reputation.

Process

Negative community perceptions, such as feelings of being insensitive to a community's needs, may damage an organization's good reputation. Since people naturally dislike conflict, especially conflict that has the potential to escalate to violence, violent encounters between security personnel and uncooperative subjects have the potential to harm an organization's reputation. No matter how well organizations manage conflict, there will be occasions when interpersonal field conflict escalates to violence and an organization's response to it has the potential to create controversy and damage its reputation.

Reputation as an Intangible Asset

According to George Nuefeld, an expert in organizational risk management, a solid reputation is necessary for maintaining financial viability. In the September 2007 issue of *Risk Management Magazine*, in an article titled, "Managing Reputation Risk," Nuefeld argues that an organization's reputation is an *intangible asset* that accounts for 70% of its value (Nuefeld, 2007 p. 70). Nuefeld summarizes a 2005 report by the Economist Intelligence Unit (EUI), entitled "Reputation: Risk of Risks." The EUI's report is based on survey input from 269 risk managers in companies of various sizes. The report lists five assumptions about the importance of maintaining a solid business reputation:

1. Corporate reputation is a hugely valuable asset that needs to be protected.
2. Serious reputational damage can occur simply as a result of perceived failures, even if those perceptions are not grounded in fact.
3. Understanding how different aspects of an organization's activities impinge on stakeholder perceptions is a vital aspect of protecting a company's reputation.
4. Many companies feel that their capabilities in managing reputational risk leave much room for improvement, but the high rewards of success should provide strong motivation for progress in this area.
5. Incurring reputational damage can be fatal, but establishing a robust reputation can provide a strong competitive advantage.

These five business imperatives demonstrate how valuable an organization's reputation is and how important it is to protect it. Reputation protection needs to include protection from attacks associated with attempts to resolve interpersonal field conflict.

Is Perception Reality?

"Perception is reality," as the adage goes. No conflict resolution strategy can succeed if a large portion of the community perceives it as ineffective or abusive. Alienating large blocks of organizational stakeholders or community members makes it much more difficult for organizations to accomplish their organizational safety goals. A successful conflict resolution strategy should include a strong focus on organizational safety education and conflict perception management. Community members that understand the rationale behind their organization's conflict resolution strategies are more likely to support and defend their choices, especially during times of crisis.

Organizations that fail to implement a comprehensive strategy to manage the public's perception of their conflict resolution strategies might not be able to successfully protect their reputation when they're publically challenged. Without a comprehensive strategy, organizations could find themselves under the scrutiny of the mass media, without the ability to defend themselves. Unfortunately, once the media starts focusing on an organization, it's too late to manage perceptions; the organization is then forced to shift valuable resources and energy to reputation damage control. Many organizations never recover from the costs associated with being forced to redirect their limited resources from running their business operations to damage control.

Community Sensitivities

Organizational and community members have varied sensitivities toward using physical force (or failure to use force) to resolve interpersonal field conflict. Universally, there's strong support for theories of conflict resolution, but not always in their application (especially when physical force is used); offended parties may react in a very public manner. Since many people believe in a forceless approach to conflict resolution, reinforced by the mass media, society, peers, and even some employers, it's important to educate the community on an organization's rationale and justification for its preferred conflict resolution strategies. It's not uncommon for community members to voice their disapproval of the strategies used after security personnel are involved in a critical field interaction.[1] In some communities, security personnel are

---

[1] Critical field interactions are defined as interactions between security personnel and resistant individuals that result in physical injuries or a catastrophic event.

perceived as not assertive enough; in others, even talking to a person in a firm voice could generate a complaint about personnel! It's understandable, but not good policy, when organizations overreact to challenges of their conflict resolution strategies and make rash changes to them. In many cases these complaints are the result of poor organizational leadership and a lack of information about an organization's corporate approach to conflict resolution, not in the actual use of a particular strategy.

When security personnel are observed in critical interactions with uncooperative individuals, community members make judgments (uncritical) about the involved participants (Thompson, 2009 p. 1577). These judgments form the basis for how the community members perceive their organization's security personnel. There are no *neutral* perceptions of critical interactions; everyone takes a side! Today when there's a physical altercation between uniformed personnel, including police or security personnel, and resistant subjects, community judgments (especially the initial ones) tend to be critical of the authority figure or uniformed individual.[2]

In the past when community members witnessed an altercation between a uniformed individual and a resistant subject, there may have been a bias in favor of the uniformed individual (the authority figure) and against the resistant subject. The general assumption used to be that the resistant subject probably deserved the type of treatment he or she was receiving from the uniformed individual. Today, because of the media's influence, including YouTube, and leadership failures in the criminal justice system, *observer bias effect* (OBE) seems to be solidly *against* authority figures (uniformed personnel). The most likely public response to these types of interactions is to assume that the uniformed individual overreacted.

Although this observer bias effect is not new, we've recently noticed two quantifiable and associated trends. One trend is a greater willingness of community members (and the mass media) to assume that the uniformed individual is at fault. In other words, some assume that personnel are probably abusing their authority; these conclusions are determined without any discernible facts to support them. The other is an overemphasis on cultural, ethic, racial, and gender-related factors thought to motivate a uniformed individual's decisions to use physical force on a resistant subject.[3]

Protection Strategies for Your Reputation

Absent a strategy, it's difficult for organizations to stand up to community pressure that inevitably comes after a critical field interaction between security personnel

---

[2]During the initial phase of an actual physical altercation, members of the public may not differentiate between security personnel and police officers, especially in organizations where security personnel dress like police officers.

[3]The mass media's response to the shooting death of Trayvon Martin on February 26, 2012, in Florida is one example.

and uncooperative subjects. Unfortunately, some organizations believe it's important to assuage the community *every time* they're challenged. Every organization needs to have a systematic approach for evaluating challenges to its security personnel's conflict resolution decisions. Constantly apologizing or kowtowing to community members also makes it more challenging for security personnel to resolve future conflict, because it reinforces the perception (or reality) that security personnel, or their organizational safety mission, lack organizational authority or value. Successful organizational safety programs depend on high levels of understanding and *tacit* agreements among senior stakeholders, organizational members, customers, and visitors. Establishing cooperative partnerships with these various stakeholder groups helps protect an organization's reputation.

Education is another impart component of reputation protection. Organizations should educate employees and community members on their standards for acceptable behavior and their approved conflict resolution strategies for dealing with violators. Organizations should also maintain an *active* organizational safety public relations campaign and have a comprehensive organizational safety crisis communication plan in place to effectively confront reputation attacks.

No one who frequents an organization should be surprised to learn that their behavior violates a community's standard, especially when individuals are uncooperative. If security personnel are responsible for protecting organizational members from harm, their role and methods for resolving conflict should be clearly articulated to all organizational and community members. If an organization's reputation is challenged after a critical field interaction between security personnel and an uncooperative subject, a lack of clarity on the security personnel's role in the conflict resolution process is a vulnerable area for a reputation attack.

To protect their organization, stakeholders must be able to document and demonstrate that individual violators were aware of the community standard, the consequences for violating it, and the role and methods of an organization's security personnel in resolving conflict. Next, there needs to be a clear and defendable pattern demonstrating that uncooperative individuals are treated fairly and consequences for inappropriate behavior have been consistently applied. Finally, the security department needs an internal system for holding security personnel accountable for their protective action choices.[4]

Conflict Resolution in Reputation Management

Organizations should communicate their conflict resolution strategies to all stakeholders in unambiguous ways. In many organizations there's a mystery surrounding

---

[4] See Chapter 12 for a detailed exposition of accountability.

security personnel and the security department's role in the conflict resolution process. (Unfortunately, if a critical field interaction becomes public, this mystery may turn into a legal thriller!) Demystifying or personalizing the security department, its role, its methods, and its personnel will improve an organization's ability to defend against a reputation attack. Since security personnel are often seen as spoil sports, the better integrated they are into other organizational stakeholder groups, the more difficult it will be to develop negative perceptions, especially if security personnel are involved in a critical field interaction.

An organization's use-of-force policies and procedures and the acceptable methods for resolving conflict should be communicated to all internal and external stakeholders. Again, transparency is the best defense against an allegation of inappropriate use of physical force. As an example, if an individual were to complain he was "tased" by security personnel and the community was unaware that their organization's security personnel carried *Tasers,* this surprise, not necessarily the *tasing,* could be the impetus for shifting public opinion against the organization.

The Public Relations Campaign: A Key Tool

Many organizations regularly promote aspects of their organization, product, or service to their organizational and community members and the general public, but rarely do they highlight the achievements of their individual stakeholder groups or departmental personnel. Organizations need to expand their current public relations campaign to include an ongoing campaign to create, promote, and maintain positive public images of their organization's organizational safety programs, their conflict resolution strategies, and their security personnel. The goal is to create positive perceptions of the personnel that may be involved in critical field interactions. Since most security personnel work 24/7/365, there are numerous and regular opportunities for a public relations campaign to promote and highlight the good deeds their security personnel regularly perform.

The Important Role in Crisis Communication

Organizations need a *systematic* crisis communication strategy to manage crises and respond to public challenges to their reputations. Crisis communication management plays an important role in successful conflict resolution and reputation protection. Every organization needs to have trained members of the organization (or the responsibility could be outsourced to a reliable vendor) who are responsible for coordinating the organization's crisis communication concerns. In this instant-media age, even YouTube videos filmed and posted by *nonaffiliated* individuals could have a devastating impact on an organization's reputation and its ability to remain competitive and profitable, especially if it's unprepared to respond to attacks on its public image.

The reality is that every organization, especially organizations that take a proactive approach to organizational safety and conflict resolution, will be involved in some type of critical field interaction that may generate unwanted public attention. Although there are many different types of public attacks to an organization's reputation, including investigations by governmental agencies, allegations of criminal wrongdoing, media inquiries, and civil lawsuits or employee wrongdoing, our primary concern is responding to public challenges to an organization's conflict resolution strategies when force (or protective action) is used by security personnel.

Failure to Manage Perceptions

An organization that fails to manage the public's impressions of its organizational safety programs *will* generate unwanted public attention that will distract from the organization's primary business functions, causing it irreparable harm and negatively impacting its ability to remain financially viable in its market.

There are thousands of representative examples whereby organizations failed to manage their community's perceptions *after* a critical field interaction between first-responder personnel and community members that resulted in irreversible damage to the organization's public reputation.

Examples from Today's Headlines

HEADLINE: "CHINESE STUDENTS GRILL USC, LAPD, REPS ON SHOOTING AND SECURITY ISSUES"

On April 9, 2012, two international students were shot and killed while sitting in their car just outside the University of Southern California (USC) campus in Los Angeles. Many in the USC community were not happy with the Los Angeles Police Department (LAPD) and USC campus security department response to these murders. On April 17, 2012, the university community and local law enforcement met to talk about the community's concerns. Several people attending the meeting voiced concerns about security, whereas others said they would transfer to a safer campus (Zheng, 2012). The parents of the two slain students subsequently filed a multimillion-dollar wrongful-death lawsuit against the USC (Winton, 2012).

In an *Los Angeles Times* online article, "USC Hopes Slayings Won't Hurt Foreign Enrollment," Barmak Nassirian, an official at the American Association of Collegiate Registrars and Admissions Officers, stated, "What may have been a very random event may turn into an impression that Southern California is not safe in general, whether that's accurate or not" (Gordon, 2012a,b). Whether the USC campus is actually safe may depend more on *how* the university manages the community's perception of these senseless killings than on the actual community safety facts!

HEADLINE: "OFFICERS DID NOTHING TO HELP"

On January 28, 2010, two juvenile subjects were videotaped fighting in the Seattle bus terminal while three uniformed security officers stood by and failed to intervene. This video went viral on the Internet and brought worldwide attention to Seattle and to the organization that employed the security officers. The community was outraged because the security personnel were perceived as doing nothing while a young girl was being savagely beaten. The video shows one of the combatants being knocked to the ground while a suspect continually kicks a young girl in the face, and the security officers stand nearby and fail to intervene.

After the video went viral, the security company and the city were sued for failing to act to protect the victim. This interaction ignited a debate about the validity of *observe and report* (OR) policies. The organization was embarrassed because of the worldwide community outrage at the organization's policy that forbade uniformed first responders from protecting a person from being attacked. The public's response to this interaction and the organization's poor public response damaged this organization's reputation beyond repair.

HEADLINE: "OFFICERS PEPPER-SPRAY PEACEFUL PROTESTORS!"

On November 11, 2011, a University of California (UC) Davis campus police officer pepper-sprayed protestors that were blocking a public walkway. The interaction was videotaped and posted online. After the videotape of the interaction went viral, there was an enormous public outcry alleging that the police officer who sprayed the individuals acted in a *criminal manner* when he pepper-sprayed the nonviolent protestors. This interaction created a public relations battle between the UC Davis administration, the UC Davis Police Department, and the public. The public eventually sided with the UC Davis administration and the protestors. Police Chief Annette M. Spicuzza subsequently resigned and other police officers were suspended (Gordon, 2011). On September 26, 2012, the university settled a lawsuit for $1 million brought by the affected protestors who alleged the officers used "excessive force," (Caesar). In the end this case cost the UC system over $2.5 million: $1 million for legal fees, $500,000 to investigate it, and $1 million to settle with the thirty plaintiffs.

These are only three examples among thousands in which an organization failed to effectively manage its community's perceptions of interpersonal field conflict, leading to a loss in reputation. The experience and wisdom gained from these interactions (and many others) and the public's reaction to these types of interactions need to influence an organization and their security personnel's conflict decision-making process.

Summary

Responsible organizations need to do their best to create safe and secure environments where conflict and violence are minimized. However, organizations also have to anticipate and manage how the public will respond to their security personnel and their conflict resolution strategies especially when personnel are involved in critical field interactions. No matter how well organizations resolve interpersonal field conflict, there will be occasions when security personnel will interact with violent individuals and have no choice but to use protective action to resolve it. These responses have the potential to save lives, but they also have the potential to damage an organization's reputation.

RECOMMENDATIONS

1. Educate organizational and community members on the organization's organizational safety expectations.
2. Educate both internal and external stakeholders on the roles and responsibilities that security personnel play in the conflict resolution process.
3. Create a corporate safety public relations program that highlights the positive attributes of the organization's security personnel and their approved field conflict resolution strategies.
4. Develop a comprehensive crisis communication strategy to manage the community's response to security personnel's conflict resolution choices.

References

Ceasar, S., 2012. UC reaches pepper spray deal. B2, Los Angeles Times, 26.09.12.

Gordon, L., 2012a. USC hopes slaying won't hurt foreign enrollment. Los Angeles Times, 14 April 2012;Web: < www.latimes.com > 07.07.12.

Gordon, L., 2012b. UC Davis police chief quits after critical report on pepper spraying. LA Now, Los Angeles Times, < www.latimesblogs.com > 12.07.12.

Nuefeld, G., 2007. Managing reputation risk. Risk Resolut. Mag. 54, 70–79.

Thompson, W.C., 2009. Interpretation: observer effects. In: Jamieson, A., Moenssens, A. (Eds.), Wiley Encyclopedia of Forensic Science Wiley, Chichester, UK, pp. 1575–1579.

Winton, R., 2012. Parents of two slain Chinese students sue USC. Los Angeles Times, 18 May 2012; Web: < www.latimes.com > 02.07.12.

Zheng, G., 2012. Chinese students grill USC, LAPD reps on shooting and security issues. USC Annenberg Digital News, 17 May 2012; Web: < www.neontommy.com > 04.07.12.

Policies

Chapter 6

Developing Policies on Conflict and Violence

The Problem

Organizations are unable to formulate effective conflict resolution policies to protect organizational and community members from inevitable, unavoidable, and unpredictable personal interactions.

Introduction

Policies that guide an organization's security personnel's actions for protecting individuals from uncooperative, dangerous, or violent individuals need to be based on realistic assumptions about the nature of conflict, conflict makers, and effective conflict resolution methods. Since conflict is inevitable, unavoidable, and unpredictable, security personnel need access to a full spectrum of conflict resolution strategies to effectively resolve it.

Any time more than one human gathers anywhere, there's always the potential for interpersonal field conflict. Since conflict always has the potential to escalate to violence, responsible organizations need to enact effective conflict resolution strategies to mitigate the potentiality of simple conflict escalating to violence.

55

Process

Many organizations base their conflict resolution policies on a flawed understanding of conflict, violence, and safety. Safety is not the absence of conflict; rather, it is effectively managed conflict. This basic misunderstanding of interpersonal field conflict and violence create a false belief that violence can be avoided or assuaged without the need for security personnel to ever use protective action to resolve it. Unfortunately, these beliefs lead to the creation of ineffective use-of-force policies that result in decreases in personnel and organizational safety and increases in potential violence and liabilities.

How Can Conflict Resolution Be Incorporated into Organizational Policies?

Strictly defined, *conflict* is an expressed struggle between at least two interdependent parties who perceive incompatible goals, scarce resources, and interference from the other party in achieving their goals (Wilmot and Hocker, 2007 p. 102). However, from a *protective* organizational safety perspective, *conflict* is defined as a unique type of interpersonal field conflict that occurs when individuals violate an organization's behavioral standard and the behavior has the potential to create physical harm.

Viewing Conflict Resolution as a Unique Business Task

Managing and resolving conflict is unlike any other regularly performed organizational task. The most obvious reason for this is that it involves deliberately placing a small cadre of employees in possible physical danger in order to protect others. This fact is often overlooked or minimized in discussing conflict and conflict resolution strategies. Unlike other employees or community members, security personnel choose to run toward potentially dangerous situations while most others run from them. Moreover, when interpersonal conflict becomes unbearable, "security" is called to resolve it. There are also unique challenges associated with managing a process that never sleeps. Security personnel are typically the only organizational stakeholder group that performs their job responsibilities 24/7/365 and on every major holiday. Since conflict can't be avoided or appeased in all cases, organizations need reliable conflict resolution strategies that allow personnel a wide array of options, including the use of protective action.

Security personnel interact with potentially uncooperative subjects in two basic conflict contexts: *directed or initiated*:

1. Personnel are *directed* to *reported* interactions that involve organizational safety violations that have the potential to lead to physical harm.

2. Personnel *initiate* contact with individuals whom they observe violating the community standard that has the potential to lead to physical harm.

There are many types of behavior that may violate an organization's behavioral standard; some violate the law, whereas others may simply violate a company policy. However, our primary focus is on managing and resolving interpersonal field conflict that has the potential to create physical injuries. We realize there are many other types of unacceptable behavior that may violate a community standard, but our focus is on mitigating behaviors that create unsafe conditions for customers, employees, and visitors.[1]

Two most common responses from subjects confronted by authority figures are passive-aggressiveness and direct aggression. Sometimes passive-aggressive or directly aggressive individuals become physically assaultive when advised by security personnel to stop behavior that may create physical harm. Although most aggressive encounters can be managed by trained professional security personnel with good communication skills, some conflict can only be resolved safely through physical intervention.

Potentiality and Complacency

The most effective way to minimize conflict's potentiality is for trained security personnel to apply effective conflict resolution strategies before conflict escalates to violence. In fact, even relatively safe organizations are not immune from the potentiality of simple interpersonal field conflict escalating to violence. Low-conflict environments have some unique and additional challenges compared to historically high-conflict or less safe environments. In low-conflict environments where conflict is rare and violence is even rarer, complacency can create a false sense of safety for community members and security personnel. Unlike low-conflict environments, high-conflict environments provide regular opportunities for security personnel to interact with conflict makers and develop a better understanding of conflict's potentiality. Complacency, created by the infrequency of interpersonal field conflict, also creates additional training challenges for organizations and security personnel.

Unfortunately, these "so-called" *peaceful* environments also lull senior stakeholders into a false belief that it's *not necessary* to invest in organizational safety, professional security personnel, or security personnel training.

At this point in our social evolution, there's no need to make an exhaustive list of the thousands of violent interactions that have already taken place in "so-called" *safe communities* where there was a low probability of anything bad happening.

---

[1] See Chapter 3 for a more detailed exposition of protective community safety principles.

CASE EXAMPLES: WHY POLICY IS IMPORTANT

These following examples are stark reminders of the potential dangers that every organization faces.

October 12, 2011: Salon Meritage, in Seal Beach, California; eight killed.

February 22, 2012: Five people were killed in a Korean health spa in Norcross, Georgia.

February 26, 2012: Multiple gunmen began firing into a nightclub crowd in Jackson, Tennessee, killing one person and injuring 20 others.

February 27, 2012: Three students at Chardon High School in rural Ohio were killed when a classmate opened fire.

March 8, 2012: Two people were killed and seven wounded at a psychiatric hospital in Pittsburgh, Pennsylvania, when a gunman entered the hospital with two semiautomatic handguns and began firing.

March 31, 2012: A gunman opened fire on a crowd of mourners at a North Miami, Florida, funeral home, killing two people and injuring 12 others.

April 2, 2012: A 43-year-old former student at Oikos University in Oakland, California, walked into his former school and killed seven people, "execution-style." Three people were wounded.

April 6, 2012: Two men went on a deadly shooting spree in Tulsa, Oklahoma; three men died and two were wounded.

May 29, 2012: A man in Seattle, Washington, opened fire in a coffee shop and killed five people and then himself.

July 9, 2012: Three people were killed at a soccer tournament in Wilmington, Delaware, including a 16-year-old player and the event organizer, when multiple gunmen began firing shots, apparently targeting the organizer.

July 20, 2012: James Holmes entered a midnight screening of *The Dark Knight Rises* and opened fire with a semi-automatic weapon; 12 people were killed and 58 wounded.

August 5, 2012: A white supremacist and former Army veteran shot six people to death inside a Sikh temple in suburban Milwaukee, Wisconsin, before killing himself.

August 14, 2012: Three people were killed at Texas A&M University when a 35-year-old man went on a shooting rampage; one of the dead was a police officer.

September 27, 2012: A 36-year-old man who had just been laid off from Accent Signage Systems in Minneapolis, Minnesota, entered his former workplace and shot five people to death and wounded three others before killing himself.

October 21, 2012: Forty-five-year-old Radcliffe Franklin Haughton shot three women to death, including his wife, Zina Haughton, and injured four others at a spa in Brookfield, Wisconsin, before killing himself.

December 11, 2012: A 22-year-old began shooting at random at a mall near Portland, Oregon, killing two people and then himself.

December 14, 2012: Adam Lanza murdered 26 people at Sandy Hook Elementary School in Newtown, Connecticut, including 20 children, before killing himself.

It's obvious from these and the many other violent interactions that no community is immune from an act of violence. Professional security personnel play an important role in resolving conflict and protecting organizational and community members.

Whose Force is Best?

Even organizations that have a solid understanding of violence and conflict are still unconvinced that security personnel should be allowed to use protective action as an option to resolve conflict. Many senior stakeholders believe that *only* law enforcement personnel should use physical force to resolve conflict. They argue that security personnel, unlike law enforcement officers, *create* rather than *mitigate* liability when they use physical strategies to resolve conflict. It's true that law enforcement personnel are generally immune from liability when they use force in the scope of their employment.[2] Although private security personnel don't have these same protections, a fair comparison (a calculated-risk assessment) needs to take into account the *total* liabilities of using physical force to resolve conflict, not just potential liabilities associated with taking action.

The Role of "Response Time"

Unlike law enforcement officers, security personnel have the distinct advantage of being *on site* when a conflict occurs, and they're usually the first stakeholders to arrive at the scene. Since time plays an important role in resolving conflict and protecting people, being in proximity to the conflict gives security personnel a unique advantage over law enforcement personnel.[3] A shorter response time has the potential to provide individuals higher levels of physical protection while simultaneously mitigating potential liability associated with negligence. The recent Sandy Hook school murders in Newton, Connecticut, is a stark reminder of the role that time plays in the conflict resolution process. It took Adam Lanza about four minutes to kill 20 children![4]

"Force" as a Normative Business Strategy

When properly applied, *protective action* is a useful business strategy that helps businesses create safe organizations and protects individuals from dangerous or violent individuals. The simple truth is that to maintain the safest and most secure organizations possible, there will be occasions when it's necessary to force individuals to correct their physically harmful behavior because it's in the best interest of the entire community.

---

[2] California Penal Code 148 (a), 834 (a), and 836.6 (a) are a few examples.
[3] Security personnel also know their community's geography better than responding personnel!
[4] A total of 26 people were killed. It took the police approximately eight minutes to arrive on the scene.

In a perfect world, when individuals are confronted about their potentially harmful behavior, they would simply correct it and be grateful that it was brought to their attention. However, today more seemingly simple conflict often ends up escalating to violence. Too many individuals are seemingly becoming more resistant to being asked to do even the simplest tasks, such as adjusting their potentially harmful behavior to conform to an organization's community standard. Unfortunately, some organizations abdicate their responsibility by appeasing conflict makers, which ultimately backfires by emboldening more potentially harmful behavior and in the end creates a greater potential for simple conflict to escalate to violence.

Forceless Organizational Safety

As difficult as this is for some people to believe, it's impossible to resolve conflict without occasionally resorting to the use of physical conflict resolution strategies. There's no perfect *forceless* strategy that can stop some individuals from being physical threats.

There are only two ways to make people behave correctly: Create an environment where reasonable people are likely to *voluntarily submit* to an organization's behavioral standard and hope they'll do so, or physically contain them when they fail to follow the standard. Although many of these violations should be managed by law enforcement personnel, it's naïve (and dangerous) to think that all violent encounters could (or should) be managed by calling the local police and waiting for them to save the day.

Talk is Not Enough

No sensible individual prefers managing or resolving conflict using physical means. There are many reasons to prefer *talk* over physical means; it's safer for personnel, for resistant individuals, and for the community. In fact, when security personnel are trained in verbal tactics,[5] fewer interpersonal field conflicts escalate to the point of *needing* to be resolved with physical strategies. However, when talk isn't effective or there are exigent circumstances, victims of violence can't wait for the police to respond to save them; security personnel should be empowered to act.

The Role of Security Professionals

Organizations that utilize security personnel to maintain safe environments typically recruit and employ individuals who have a passion for helping others. Security personnel have a natural affinity for protecting victims from criminal behavior. Security individuals have chosen to work the security profession because it affords them opportunities to help people in distress. For these individuals, it's

---

[5] See Chapter 10 for a more detailed exposition of verbal tactics.

extremely difficult and counterintuitive to be constrained by policies that forbid them from acting to protect distressed community members. It's also unrealistic to expect these personality types, who are drawn to the helping professions, to stand by while people within their reach are being victimized. Security personnel intuitively know that their simplest actions would likely protect individuals from being victimized.

In fact, even when there are *explicit* policies forbidding security personnel from getting involved, ethical individuals will act anyway, because their personal character and integrity dictate it. There's no policy that will stop security personnel from protecting themselves from physical harm and, in many cases, from coming to the aid of others who are being victimized. One practical outcome of noncontact or overly restrictive use-of-force policies is making ethical individuals into lawbreakers! The only way to create ethical and responsible security personnel behavior is to enact *situational* use-of-force subject contact policies[6] enabled by reliable training programs.

Summary

Organizations must base their conflict resolution strategies and policies on a realistic understanding of conflict and violence as well as the unique challenges security personnel face in the conflict resolution process. Since conflict is inevitable, unavoidable, unpredictable, and rare, organizations need to allow for a full spectrum of conflict resolution strategies.

RECOMMENDATIONS

1. Educate all organizational stakeholders on the realities, difficulties, and responsibilities of resolving conflict and maintaining safe organizations.
2. Utilize reality-based conflict models for developing appropriate and effective conflict resolution strategies.

Reference

Wilmot, W.W., Hocket, J.L., 2007. Interpersonal Field Conflict, seventh ed. McGraw-Hill, New York.

---

[6]Situational use-of-force subject contact policies allow personnel to decide the best protective option based on the totality of the circumstances known to them at the time of the field conflict.

Chapter 7

Use-of-Force Policies and Risk Mitigation

The Problem

Organizations are unable to formulate effective policies that guide their security personnel's physical interactions with uncooperative subjects without creating unreasonable financial and civil exposure.

Introduction

Use-of-force policies[1] that guide security personnel actions for physically interacting with uncooperative, dangerous, or violent individuals are necessary for resolving

---

[1] Although the term *use of force* is the most widely used term to describe interactions between security personnel and resistant subjects, we prefer the term *protective action*. There are two primary reasons for this preference: (1) we think *use of force* is a term carried over from the law enforcement community and (2) *protective action* is a more accurate description of private security personnel activities. Since some readers are unfamiliar with the term *protective action*, throughout the book we'll use these two terms *use of force* and *protective action* interchangeably.

conflict, creating safe organizations, and mitigating total liabilities. Unfortunately, in the private market there's no policy that can mitigate an organization's total liability to zero. In a free market, even when an employee acts within policy, the employee and the employer can still be civilly sued. To protect themselves, successful organizations must enact conflict resolution policies that create the safest organizations possible while affording the highest levels of protection against total liabilities, not just civil liabilities associated with taking action.

Unfortunately, many organizations focus exclusively (or obsessively) on policies that attempt to mitigate civil liabilities associated with security personnel taking action, while ignoring (or minimizing) other just as potentially damaging liabilities, such as protecting their reputation or their ability to compete in their unique market. Therefore, policies that guide personnel's physical interactions with uncooperative subjects, whether they restrain or allow certain behaviors, need to be geared toward creating outcomes that have the greatest *total* benefit for the organization.

Unlike other human behaviors that organizations attempt to manage, conflict resolution activities are some of the most complicated because they involve unpredictable and highly emotional interactions. Unfortunately, most organizations respond to these conflict resolution realities in a variety of ineffective and unproductive ways. The most typical response is to enact rules-based, use-of-force policies that are narrowly focused on risk aversion.

Risk aversion policies may mitigate liability associated with some types of negligence, but they have the unintended consequence of increasing total liabilities, such as damaging an organization's reputation; creating unsafe conditions for personnel, employees, and community members; and negatively impacting personnel productivity.

Many organizations use an observe-and-report organizational safety model,[2] a risk-aversive model that prohibits or severely restricts security personnel from making physical contact[3] with uncooperative, dangerous, or violent individuals.

Process

THE ROLE OF POLICIES IN CONFLICT RESOLUTION STRATEGIES

Some organizations, whether they clearly state it or it is implied, communicate a zero-tolerance use-of-force philosophy toward any security personnel behavior that

---

[2] See Chapter 3 for a more detailed exposition of the observe-and-report community safety model.
[3] Physical contact can be made through actual hands-on behavior or through the use of a protective or defensive device or tool.

may generate potential civil liability. Many organizations use this zero-tolerance liability fallacy as the basis for developing subject contact use-of-force policies. Since no policy or procedure, no matter how well written or executed, can limit an organization's total liabilities to zero nor stop security personnel from intervening under all conditions, prohibiting intervention is unrealistic, impractical and ineffective.

Effective conflict resolution policies need to *discourage* certain behaviors, but not all behaviors, while *encouraging* other behaviors.

Many organizations live in a constant state of denial when it comes to violence and the effectiveness of their approved conflict resolution strategies. Unbelievably, some organizations even argue that they have *no* interpersonal field conflict that needs to be resolved; for them, any discussion about using *physical* conflict resolution strategies is moot! In other words, some stakeholders can't even envision *any* circumstances in which employees would need to use physical force to resolve conflict. However, I've been told that in the unlikely event that conflict finds their personnel, they'll simply call the police. Unfortunately, by the time police arrive on the scene, victims may be seriously injured and the organization's reputation destroyed. Since conflict is *inevitable, unpredictable, and unavoidable,* organizations have only two realistic options: manage it or allow it to manage them.

As a security company owner, security consultant, and security trainer, I have found convincing senior nonsecurity stakeholders to consider the business merits of allowing their security personnel to use physical conflict resolution strategies as one option of an effective conflict resolution program has been an uphill battle! Many of my conversations end up in "lawyerese," where I am eventually informed of the merits of forceless policies (such as observe-and-report organizational safety models) that have inherent powers to resolve conflict, whereas any real discussion of the benefits of allowing personnel the option of using protective action is summarily dismissed.

The primary reason organizations enact these *noncontact* use-of-force policies is that they don't trust their security personnel. First, organizations don't trust their security personnel (or their senior security managers) to act responsibly under high-stress interpersonal field conflict situations. Many fear that if personnel are given too much leeway for using physical conflict resolution strategies, they'll regularly resort to the most extreme physical options, even when dealing with low levels of interpersonal field conflict. Second, some managers believe that if they forbid or severely restrict personnel from using physical strategies to resolve conflict, personnel will never use them.

The truth is, empowering professional security personnel to use physical conflict resolution strategies as *one* of their many options for resolving conflict, within the framework of a comprehensive safety program, is an excellent *business* decision.

POLICY CONSIDERATIONS

The process of developing appropriate boundaries for security personnel involves both logical and emotional considerations. Unfortunately, it's easy for some senior stakeholders to imagine that any physical interaction between security personnel and uncooperative subjects will end up in an all-out brawl and create unnecessary liability.

However, the only effective way to successfully mitigate the *total* liabilities associated with resolving conflict with uncooperative individuals is to train security personnel in the use of protective theories, techniques, tactics, and tools and provide personnel reasonable and situational boundaries for their use.

TYPES OF POLICIES AND THEIR FOUNDATIONS

There are two types of subject contact, use-of-force policies: rules-governed or situational. However, the vast majority of organizations that employ security personnel use *rules-governed* subject contact policies within a framework of a risk-aversive, observe-and-report community safely model.

Rules-Governed Policies

There are various types of noncontact policies that are typically used in the private security industry. Noncontact policies range from strict to self-defense only. *Strict* hands-off versions typically forbid *any* physical contact between employees and uncooperative subjects, whereas *self-defense-only* policies usually allow security personnel to use physical force to only defend *themselves* against an assault.

The use of rules-governed policies tries to create an exhaustive list of "if-then" conflict resolution scenarios that predetermine their security personnel's authorized options. For instance, *if* a criminal tries to punch a security officer in the face, *then* the security officer is allowed to use pepper spray to repel the attack. However, because it's impossible to account for every possible type of resistant subject and security officer interaction, especially applied to highly emotional and extremely fluid human interactions, rules-governed policies are ineffective at resolving interpersonal field conflict and they decrease safety for both the resistant subject and the security personnel.

Rules-governed subject contact policies increase potential civil liability. Since it's virtually impossible for personnel to adhere *precisely* to "if-then" subject contact policies during actual (versus hypothetic) subject interactions, the failure to precisely follow an organization's official use-of-force policy could be used against security personnel and an organization in a lawsuit as proof that they acted improperly. In fact, defense attorneys love to cross-examine security personnel by asking them to read the "highlighted portions" of their subject contact use-of-force policy, in an attempt to demonstrate that the security personnel's behavior violated their organization's official policy.

Situational Policies

Unlike rules-governed policies, *situational* subject contact use-of-force policies provide security personnel a broad range of options for dealing with the various types of interpersonal field conflict they may face. Situational-based subject contact policies are affirmative policies that take into consideration the totality of associated risk, not just the risk of taking action to protect individuals. When security personnel are faced with a unique interpersonal field conflict scenario and use situational use-of-force policies, they're better able to quickly calculate the level of risk they face and efficiently choose the best risk/benefit option from among all their available options and successfully resolve the conflict.

The truth is, even when it's authorized, security personnel rarely ever use protective action. This infrequency makes it even more difficult for some stakeholders to understand why it's ever necessary. First, since most organizations don't operate in a war zone and have the support of their local law enforcement agency, there aren't a high number of aggressive conflict interactions that need to be resolved with physical force. In fact, even in organizations where there are a high number of conflict opportunities, the use of protective action is still a rarity because its use is only authorized under very narrow circumstances. Finally, some security personnel refuse to use physical conflict resolution strategies under any circumstance because they believe they'll get fired! Many organizational stakeholders have created an "atmosphere of fear," through both direct and indirect means, that personnel will be fired for using *any* level of force, even if they act within policy.

In what is thought to be a highly unusual response to a critical field incident with physical injuries, a hospital security officer killed a subject while attempting to resolve conflict, and his organization (Cavatti, 2011) defended him. While working as a uniformed security guard at WellStar Cobb Hospital in Austell, Georgia, Jerry Evans got into a physical altercation with a patient, and the patient subsequently died. Evans was subsequently arrested and charged with involuntary manslaughter and reckless conduct. However, after reviewing surveillance video and conducting an internal investigation, the hospital's senior stakeholders determined that Evans wasn't at fault, nor did he violate any organizational policies. The hospital decided to defend Evans and even helped him obtain an attorney.

Unlike that interaction, senior stakeholders typically apply an unrealistic *hindsight analysis* to judge security personnel and subject interactions, especially to those interactions that involve injuries. Although the legal community does not support the hindsight standard, organizations often apply it to after-action subject contact inquiries and to personnel discipline.

In 1989, the U.S. Supreme Court, in *Graham v. Connor*, determined that hindsight was an unfair standard for evaluating whether police officers were justified in using physical force to subdue resistant suspects. The new legal standard for judging use-of-force decision making is totality of circumstances and reasonableness. Although the court's decision doesn't directly apply to private security personnel, we think this is the best standard for evaluating subject contact. This legal decision makes clear the unique challenges associated with making complicated and difficult subject contact decisions. The reality is that no employees in any department, including security personnel, could ever lead or manage personnel effectively if their employment status depended solely on a hindsight standard.

Organizations that use a hindsight standard to evaluate their security personnel's use-of-force decision-making process create unproductive and hesitant personnel. Since conflict is highly unpredictable, personnel need to be more focused on making the safest choice, given the unique circumstances in which they find themselves, rather than worrying about how their choices will impact their employment. This internal dissonance may create *hesitancy to act*, creating unsafe conditions for security personnel, organizational and community members.

A lack of leadership among corporate stakeholders and senior security managers feeds these use-of-force assumptions. There's a persistent and underlying fear among some stakeholders that if they authorize security personnel to use physical strategies,[4] they'll be forced to defend their security personnel's actions (not that they want to). For some senior security managers, learning that their security personnel have been involved in a physical interaction with an uncooperative subject is their worst nightmare. These incidents often force security managers into the uncomfortable position of having to defend their employees' actions to senior stakeholders[5] who are socially or politically situated much higher in the organization.

Unfortunately, these interactions and the corresponding fault-finding expeditions often lead to personnel being "thrown under the bus" to satisfy organizational, social, or political agendas. This is especially common when physical force is used to resolve aggressive field conflict and individuals are injured. Physical injuries resulting from attempts to resolve conflict naturally generate a lot of interest among various senior organizational stakeholders. However, security personnel need to be assured[6] that if they need to use force to resolve conflict and they operate within policy, their organization will stand by them.

---

[4] Another "leaderless" approach is never advocating for the use of physical conflict resolution strategies or for the use of protective or defensive devices or tools. This approach may socially or politically protect senior stakeholders, but it leaves security personnel physically vulnerable and organizational and community members vulnerable.

[5] See Chapter 2 for a more detailed exposition of the challenges associated with socio-political organizational hierarchies.

[6] Assurance needs to more than talk! Personnel need practical demonstrations of this kind of support.

Like many of my readers, I've been to several leadership seminars and read many good leadership books.[7] Unfortunately, when security personnel are socially or politically situated at the lowest levels of their organization's power structure, it's difficult to exhibit effective leadership characteristics without paying social, financial, or employment consequences. Although both security and nonsecurity stakeholders are responsible for these leadership failures, senior nonsecurity stakeholders share the greater responsibility. These leadership failures are the result of weak character on the part of the security directors' and managers' and senior nonsecurity stakeholders' inability to share social-organizational power. Unfortunately, these leadership failures are often self-fulfilling prophecies; security managers are afraid to exert leadership traits, senior nonsecurity stakeholders fail to trust their security manager's leadership abilities, and security managers socially withdraw and become timid and ineffective followers. This "leaderless" cycle is responsible for neutering many seemingly professional security managers and has subsequently created a stockpile of discarded, but competent, unemployed security professionals.

In fact, Joseph Wambaugh, the famous former LAPD detective and author, recently wrote an op-ed article for the *Los Angeles Times* in which he commented on the sociopolitical environment and the consequences of taking a leadership role in the well-publicized University of California at Davis pepper-spray case of November 2011 that led to the police chief's resignation.[8] Wambaugh wrote, "… instead of doing what most police chiefs routinely do (including Bratton) and issuing a pension-saving CYA statement and throwing her cops under the bus. That loyalty probably cost her [Spicuzza] the chief job" (Wambaugh, 2011). In the end, Spicuzza, the UC Davis police chief, resigned, and other police officers were subsequently disciplined or fired.

Part of the long-term solution to these leaderless environments is both individual and organizational. Individual security professionals need to find ways to create personal relevance in their organizations, and senior stakeholders need to encourage (and practice) the sharing of political and social power with their security department managers and directors.

Paradoxically, the cause for the resistance to share organizational power may be related to senior organizational stakeholders' preference for hiring police-oriented personnel who don't share their philosophical, educational, business, or social background. The truth is these two stakeholder groups have very little in common.

An Approach to Policy Making

Attorneys, human resource managers, risk managers, insurance providers, police managers, business executives, and even the mass media have the greatest influence

---

[7] I highly recommend the book *Leadership: Texas Hold'em Style*, by Andrew J. Harvey and Raymond E. Foster.
[8] See Larry Gordon, "UC Davis police chief quits after critical report on pepper spraying," for a more detailed exposition of these issues.

on determining an organization's approved conflict resolution policies. Unfortunately, it's rare for organizations to take their senior security personnel experiences and thoughts seriously in the development of an organization's use-of-force policy.

The undeniable truth is that it's impossible to create effective policies for any department (especially use-of-force policies) without involving the thoughts, experiences, and opinions of the end users of a policy!

Unlike other organizational processes, resolving conflict is one of the most complicated business functions that is regularly performed. Therefore, it's imperative that individuals who have actual experience dealing with aggressive individuals in a free-market security context be involved in the organization's use-of-force policy creation process. Unfortunately, stakeholders who have never been personally involved in aggressive field conflict typically make several false assumptions about the best strategies for resolving it. Two of the most common mistakes they make are an overestimation of the power of communication and an overestimation of the probability that physical intervention by security personnel will lead to serious injuries and unreasonable civil liability. Often these assumptions about the nature of conflict lead to policies that demonstrate a huge disconnect between theory and application. Unlike other departmental policies, use-of-force policies address physical harm and protective activities. Getting these policies wrong creates a false sense of safety for security personnel, and organizational and community members and increases total liabilities.

Even if it were humanly possible, with detailed policies and ongoing training and supervision, to guarantee all security personnel would actually follow noncontact use-of-force policies under all circumstances, it's still impossible to predict or control what uncooperative subjects will do. My 25 years in the security business have taught me many truths, including the certainty that security personnel or other organizational members will be physically attacked, and doing nothing will be both unethical and a poor business decision.

Shifting Liability

Even under perfect circumstances, the practical impact of noncontact or restrictive use-of-force policies is not eliminating the potential of a negligence claim or the mitigation of an actual claim; rather, they shift the primary responsibility from individuals to the organization. Even if one were to assume that any action taken by security personnel would increase civil liability because of injuries to employees or uncooperative subjects, it's just as likely that any action taken by security personnel would *mitigate* potential civil liability by eliminating or reducing potential injuries to innocent victims.

In truth, potential liability may depend more on the stakeholder *imagining* these theoretical outcomes than on *actual* outcomes.

When personnel share no responsibility for protecting community members, potential civil liability is completely shifted, transferred, or passed from the employees to the organization. There are financial costs or transfer fees associated with this shifting of responsibility.

Effective and responsible policies that guide security personnel behavior should be based on a *calculated risk,* not on a *risk aversion.* Use-of-force policies based on calculated risk create conflict resolutions outcomes that have the greatest *total* benefits for the organization, compared to outcomes based on risk aversion. Since all use-of-force choices are naturally comparative,[9] policies based on calculated risk allow personnel to choose their best available conflict resolution strategy to efficiently resolve highly volatile interpersonal field conflict.

The truth is every action or inaction by security personnel during a field conflict has the potential to either create safer or less safe conditions. A common risk aversion fallacy posits that acting naturally creates greater liabilities than inaction. In the short term, acting may in fact create some immediate legal challenges for an organization, whereas inaction may lead to future liabilities. Unlike risk-aversion policies, calculated risk-based use-of-force policies create affirmative behaviors that security personnel should take, not behaviors they should avoid.

Even if forbidding employees to act were able to minimize liability by shifting some responsibility from the employee to the organization, this shift is still more likely to increase total liabilities because of the additional costs associated with a negligence claim for failure to act. Negligence based on failure-to-act claims not only creates civil liability, it also creates negative community perceptions of the organization and damages its reputation.[10] Organizations that are perceived as insensitive to their community's safety concerns, such as failing to protect community members, damage their reputation, which in turn makes it even more difficult for the organizations to compete in their marketplace, thus creating financial instability.

Restricting or prohibiting security personnel from making physical contact with individuals may cause more problems than it solves. Use-of-force policies that forbid security personnel from making physical contact delay help from getting to potential crime victims in a timely manner. Waiting to take action is only beneficial when conflict doesn't involve the potential for physical injuries. Getting all necessary resources quickly to the scene of a field conflict can assist distressed individuals and protect life

---

[9] Use-of-force decisions are partially based on the type of training that personnel receive and the defensive or protective devices and tools they carry. In other words, personnel are limited to their "best choice" based on the tactics and tools available to them, not on options they don't possess. For example, prior to the advent of Tasers, police officers used hands-on physical force to subdue resistant subjects. Now they use Tasers that allow them to stand at a safe distance while they deploy probes that immobilize the resistant suspect. The use of a Taser, compared to the use of physical hands-on force, reduces both officer and suspect injuries.

[10] See Chapter 5 for a more detailed exposition of the costs of a damaged reputation.

and is a practical demonstration of an organization's ethical commitment to its community members.

When employees are forbidden to physically interact with uncooperative subjects, there are unintended consequences. Since all organizations have a "duty-of-care" responsibility and must maintain safe environments that protect all people who visit their property, having security personnel seemingly available to help but actually prohibited from acting may increase the potential of a negligence claim for breach of duty.

Forbidding security personnel from making physical contact also means that community members have to rely on other resources to protect them from aggressive subjects, no matter how long it takes them to arrive. Because conflict comes in varying sizes and degrees of trouble, there will naturally be some low-level conflict that security personnel could easily resolve by preventing simple interactions from becoming serious. Forbidding any physical contact between security personnel and uncooperative subjects guarantees that some simple conflict will escalate to serious conflict!

Organizational Malpractice

From the community's perspective, presenting security personnel as available but unable to help may be considered a form of organizational malpractice. When security personnel are called upon to help and they don't respond in the way that community members expect, regardless of the actual policy, the community will perceive personnel as unwilling to act to protect them. Security personnel inaction creates negative community perceptions. Community members generally interpret a lack of willingness to help a person in distress as a moral failing. Even in organizations where community members are well educated about an organization's policy that forbids physical contact by security personnel (which is rare), no community education program can override a community's natural tendency to expect Good Samaritans to come to their aid when they're in trouble.

Dealing with Conflict Resolution Expectations

When security personnel are perceived by community members as available to help but are actually prohibited from physically intervening, their expectations of service are elevated. Communities naturally expect uniformed security personnel to be able to perform many organizational safety tasks, including coming to their aid if they're being victimized. In fact, the bar is raised even higher for organizations in which uniformed security personnel dress like police officers, wear police-type duty gear, and drive police-type vehicles.[11]

---

[11] See Chapter 4 for a more detailed exposition of security personnel identity.

Besides being perceived as available to help, when security personnel dress like police officers, it further elevates community members' expectations of service. Unlike security personnel, police officers have a wide array of resources and training to help support their community safety needs. Dressing like police officers creates an expectation that uniformed security personnel should be able to perform many of the same high-level community safety tasks as police officers, *including* coming to community member's aid under very complicated and potentially violent circumstances. There's a natural relationship between perceived expectations of service and actual service. This is especially paradoxical for organizations that enact noncontact use-of-force policies *while* employing security personnel that dress and look like police officers!

From the community member's perspective, not providing the same level of service as police officers ("especially since you look like a cop…") may be perceived as a cruel joke. Failure to meet the community's expectations, especially when the community feels duped, creates negative community attitudes toward security personnel and an organization's safety program.

Although it's difficult to calculate actual loss in revenue based on negative community perceptions, there are plenty of examples where a damaged reputation based on safety concerns (failing to act or protect) was costly. For example, the LA Dodgers' organization lost millions of dollars in revenue in 2011 because a fan, Brian Stow, was severely beaten, and the assault created public perceptions that the stadium was unsafe (Dilbeck, 2011). Since many field conflict interactions can be resolved effectively with low levels of physical subject interaction, it's pragmatically and ethically difficult for organizations to defend inaction by personnel.

Under circumstances where security personnel are only allowed to be "good witnesses" rather than able to help community members, feelings of deception and mistrust are often created. In some organizations, when a problem arises, community members are required to contact security, not the police. Under some circumstances, when security personnel arrive on the scene, they're not authorized to actually help; all they can do is call the police and report the incident. The time that's wasted waiting for ineffective security personnel to arrive and access an incident, rather than it being reported directly to the police, could be the difference between a minor injury and death.

Restrictive or hands-off use-of-force polices may create underground security personnel practices. Underground policies create unintended civil and criminal liability for organizations. It's not unusual that when there's strong disagreement with an organizational policy, regardless of actual written policies, employees will often passively or actively resist them. Resistance to subject contact use-of-force policies is played out in various ways by security personnel. Passive-resistant security personnel simply become unproductive employees; they avoid *any* interaction that may involve potential conflict. On the other hand, actively resistant personnel become *overly* aggressive with subjects, to prove their organization's use-of-force policies are ineffective. Furthermore, these underground policies create an additional burden for supervisors. Supervisors have to keep *policy resisters* from developing cliques that undermine the organization's safety mission and create negative personnel morale.

Forbidding security personnel from using physical conflict resolution strategies also creates employment uncertainty. Since security personnel are constantly being placed in complicated and potentially violent interpersonal field conflict situations, they're continually challenged to make snap use-of-force decisions, sometimes choosing between ethical behaviors (self-protection) and policy compliance. This uncertainty has the potential to decrease security personnel safety because personnel are more focused on avoiding behavior that could get them fired rather than making the safest conflict resolution decision.

Moreover, *restrictive* use-of-force policies cannot protect employees, visitors, or others when they're being actively and savagely assaulted while waiting for the police to arrive. If a community member is assaulted while security personnel stand by and "do nothing," especially if the interaction is videotaped and posted on YouTube, how would it impact an organization's reputation? Community members don't react positively to an organization's decisions to forbid security personnel from helping people while they're being victimized.[12]

Summary

Risk managers are (partially) right! It's true that allowing untrained, unprofessional security personnel the option of using physical force to resolve interpersonal field conflict will increase liability. However, on balance, it's clear that when trained professional security personnel are allowed to use physical force to resolve field conflict, it creates greater total benefits than total risks for responsible organizations.

To successfully resolve field conflict, organizations need to create appropriate policies that guide their security personnel's behavior for interacting with uncooperative, dangerous, or violent individuals. In an attempt to minimize financial loss, maximize safety, and mitigate potential liability, organizations enact use-of-force policies that are thought to mitigate organizational risk. However, policies that are too narrowly focused on risk aversion and not based on calculated risk interfere with conflict resolution, increase total liabilities, and interfere with the maintenance of organizational and community safety. Effective and reliable use-of-force policies need to not only protect against potential civil liabilities but also maintain a good reputation and preserve the organization's ability to compete in their market.

---

[12] See Chapter 5 for a more detailed exposition of reputation protection.

RECOMMENDATIONS

1. Enact *situational-based* subject contact policies that allow personnel access to a full spectrum of conflict resolution strategies.
2. Use *calculated risk* to determine potential organizational risk when developing subject contact use-of-force policies.

References

Cavatti, R., 2011. Hospital backs guard accused of killing patient. WSBTV, 31 October 2011: Web: <www.wsbtv.com> 03.03.12.

Dilbeck, S., 2011. Attendance at Dodger Stadium continues to plunge. Dodger Now, Los Angeles Times, 13 May 2011; Web: <www.latimesblogs.com> 10.07.12.

Wambaugh, J., 2011. Op-Ed Columnist: Joseph Wambaugh solves the great UC Davis pepper-spraying incident. Los Angeles Times, 27 November 2011. Web: <www.articles.latimes.com>.

Section III

People as Part of a Conflict Resolution Strategy

Chapter 8

Involving People in Conflict Resolution Roles

The Problem

Organizations continue to use an ineffective employment paradigm to recruit, hire, and retain security personnel responsible for resolving field conflict and maintaining safe organizations.

Introduction

It takes unique individuals to resolve conflict involving uncooperative, dangerous, or violent individuals. The success of an organization's organizational safety program depends on employing effective and responsible personnel. Every unique department within an organization has a preferred employee profile based on certain personal characteristics, *which* may include attitude, intelligence, integrity, experience, education, or availability, to name a few. These desired, preferred, or required personal characteristics are thought to be necessary for maximizing an employee's productivity in a unique job setting. Since resolving conflict is one of the most complicated and dangerous job tasks in any organization, organizations need to be assured they're recruiting, hiring, and retaining the right individuals who *will be* responsible for making multimillion-dollar field conflict resolution decisions.

Process

An overrepresentation of police-oriented individuals[1] employed in the private security industry is an impediment to organizational safety.[2] The current employment paradigm of preferring police-oriented individuals is often thought of as both an asset and a liability for an organization. Some believe police-oriented individuals are an asset because the task of resolving interpersonal field conflict requires individuals who are physically and mentally disciplined to deal with the physical dangers associated with providing protection from violent individuals. On the other hand, police-oriented individuals may be thought of as a liability because of their tendency to overemphasize physicality as their preferred conflict resolution strategy while minimizing collaborative, more customer-focused interpersonal solutions.

However, based on the current security hiring trends, *most* senior security and nonsecurity stakeholders, corporate managers, and human resource personnel continue to believe that police-oriented employees meet their organizational needs.

However, these hiring preferences are *not* based on a rational assessment of a security employee's actual job function but are primarily the result of *unexamined* and *faulty assumptions* about the nature of private-market organizational safety principles.

The assumption that police-oriented individuals are best suited for this task is primarily the result of stakeholders' conflating the superficial similarities between these two distinct industries. The truth is there are very few actual job task similarities between law enforcement officers and private security personnel.[3] Although it's true that both these industries are generally focused on creating and maintaining safe environments, private security personnel are primarily focused on protective activities, whereas police officers focus on enforcement. These unique job task differences are nicely summarized in the book *Hospital and Healthcare Security*.

---

[1] In addition to police-oriented individuals, a significant number of former military personnel are employed in the security industry. But unlike police-oriented individuals, not all former military personnel have worked in a law enforcement capacity.

[2] The use of public law enforcement community safety philosophies is an additional impediment to organizational safety.

[3] See Chapter 2 for a more detailed exposition of these differences.

The writers define security personnel activities as organizationally defined, privately funded, and profit-driven, and they include the protection of people and property, prevention of incidents, and administrative remedies, whereas law enforcement activities are publicly defined, taxpayer-funded, and results-driven and include the enforcement of laws, apprehension of offenders, protection of society, statutorily defined, and legal remedies. The authors go on to write, "Although some common ground may exist between security and law enforcement, at least 90% of their respective activities are different" (Colling and York, 2010 p. 20).

Role Conflicts: Law Enforcement Versus Private Security

There are substantive differences between managing *private market* conflict and managing *public* conflict. The primary reasons police are successful at creating safe *public* communities are statutory authority, scope of employment immunity, extensive training, and their use of unique policing methods and tactics.[4] In fact, ask any former police officers working in private security roles and they'll provide firsthand accounts of how difficult it is to maintain safe organizations without these sworn attributes.[5] It doesn't take long for these former police officers to get their first "Welcome to the private security market, M-Effing!" Unlike private security personnel, sworn police officers have legal authority to confront verbally aggressive individuals. However, private personnel aren't given the authority, social power, or training to confront verbally abusive individuals; security personnel generally have no choice but to put up with this type of aggressive behavior.

When police officers leave the law enforcement industry, they leave behind their *authority*. Even though many police officers have extensive training résumés, their training is of little value in a private setting without its enabling statutory authority and scope of employment immunity. In fact, in a private context, law enforcement training provides no greater benefit than private security training. This is why it's counterproductive to train private security personnel in law enforcement-based peace officers standards and training (POST) instruction.[6] Without statutory authority and scope of employment immunity, it would be impossible for police officers to create safe public communities. Since private security personnel are not afforded these enabling attributes, attempts to enforce laws, policies, or rules are rarely beneficial.[7]

---

[4] See Chapter 11 for a more detailed exposition of statutory authority and scope of employment immunity.
[5] See Chapter 1 for more information on the role that setting plays in the conflict resolution process.
[6] We think POST is an excellent and useful training standard as long as the specific training does not include enforcement-based community safety principles.
[7] See Chapter 3 for a more detailed exposition of enforcement-based community safety principles.

Effective conflict resolution strategies should take into account the practical challenges of not being able to utilize statutory authority and scope of employment immunity as enabling factors for resolving private market conflict. Unfortunately, these differences have been minimized or completely ignored, creating a flawed hiring paradigm where police-oriented individuals have become the preferred private security personnel candidates.

Unlike private communities, public communities generally give police officers wide latitude in the methods and tactics they're able to use to create safe and secure communities. In fact, it's not unusual for an organization's approved conflict resolution methods and tactics to have no practical impact on organizational safety; they just happen to be the only ones acceptable to the senior stakeholders. Often organizations are more concerned with what the community finds acceptable rather than determining the most effective conflict resolution methods. For instance, in a private market, even the perception of being "too aggressive" with potential criminals may lead to negative community attitudes and a loss in market share. Conversely, being perceived as too soft on criminal behavior in the public arena may lead to increases in criminal activity and decreases in community satisfaction.

Additionally, police-oriented personnel don't typically possess the necessary private-market customer service skills or personality traits that are generally needed to process the ambiguity and the unique challenges associated with resolving interpersonal field conflict in competitive market (such as preferring verbal tactics over physical force or the use of weapons). In fact, this finding is supported by a recent University of California report.

In response to an allegation of excessive force by police officers from the University of California Davis campus, Mark G. Yudof, the University of California president, ordered a fact-finding review of the incident. One of the tentative findings reported in the "Response to Protests on UC Campuses, draft for public comment," written by University of California Dean Christopher F. Edley, Jr., and University of California General Counsel Charles F. Robinson, concluded that the UC system should hire police officers with the "right temperament" to deal with the unique challenges of managing conflict on a college campus. The authors wrote, "No matter how robust our policies are, we cannot avoid breakdowns in the police response to protests and civil disobedience if individual officers on the ground do not have the appropriate outlook and temperament" (Edley and Robinson, 2012 p. 46). In other words, even effective policies can't make up for failures to hire the right *kind* of public safety employee.

As a vocational group, police officers have been extremely effective at convincing senior organizational stakeholders that their *actual* (or perceived) law enforcement expertise provides an added benefit for their private organizations. However, we think it's time to have a serious business-minded discussion about the *true* benefits of hiring police-oriented individuals or the wisdom of using law enforcement community safety philosophies in a private setting.

In reality, there's nothing inherent about a police vocation that naturally prepares individuals for the challenges of private-market security employment. Other than some superficial similarities, such as wearing a similar uniform, working 24/7/365 shifts, and occasionally interacting with criminal behavior, these two industries are substantively dissimilar.

Paradigm Shift

Unfortunately, preferring police-oriented individuals may also contribute to security practices that are both unable to maintain high levels of organizational safety and those that interfere with an organization's primary business function. However, since senior nonsecurity stakeholders are responsible for determining their security department's mission and establishing their organization's hiring parameters, senior stakeholders share the majority of the responsibility for any operational failures, especially the decision to hire the senior security manager.[8]

Although it may seem counterintuitive, law enforcement experience may actually be an impediment to successful private-market conflict resolution. Since the vast majority of organizations prefer their security personnel not to make physical contact with uncooperative subjects, it's unrealistic to require (and expect) police-oriented individuals, who are often former police officers, to refrain from acting like police officers when they're confronted with criminal behavior.

Although there are some talented former law enforcement personnel who have made a successful transition to free-market, private security roles, we believe they are in the minority. Unfortunately, many police-oriented individuals have struggled making this transition and have failed to provide the best possible service for their organizations. My goal is not to demonize former law enforcement professionals who are doing invaluable work in the private sector. Rather, I want to challenge senior nonsecurity stakeholders to reexamine their underlying assumptions about their organizational safety philosophies and their rationale for choosing the *type* of people they believe are best suited to resolve conflict and maintain safe private communities.

My background, experience, training, credentials, and *gravitas* qualify me to speak honestly and fairly about these sensitive and controversial issues. In fact, my father and brother are both former police officers who made a successful transition from the law enforcement field to the private security market. My son and the police agency that he works for have both benefited from the time he spent working with me in the private security industry.

---

[8]Although senior nonsecurity stakeholders are responsible for hiring the senior security manager, they typically assign that individual the responsibility of hiring the remainder of the security staff. Therefore, the security manager plays an important role in hiring the "right" type of security individual.

The truth is, an honest evaluation of these issues actually benefits those who want to become police officers, those who are transitioning out of law enforcement and into the private market, and the organizations that employ them. There are many opportunities for police-oriented individuals to develop a comprehensive understanding of the organizational safety challenges that private organizations face prior to entering or leaving a law enforcement career.

"Business-Minded" Security Personnel

To effectively resolve conflict, organizations need to recruit, hire, and retain security personnel who are more like business stakeholders and less like police officers. However, there are powerful forces that will resist the shift away from police-oriented individuals to more business-minded security personnel. Change, when first proposed, is rarely embraced. But the paradigm shift away from the current hiring pattern to a more business-focused one has the potential to improve organizational safety. Initially, there may be some animosity among organizations, the security industry, and the law enforcement community. Moreover, based on today's economic realities, this may be the perfect time for organizations to start the transformational process of preferring, recruiting, and hiring business-minded individuals to fill their current and future security personnel openings.

To be clear, we are not proposing that police-oriented (or former military) personnel be disqualified from private security employment. The truth is, these individuals embody many of the required personality traits necessary for success in the private security market. However, the reason these individuals often fail is not because of poor character but because of the uniqueness of the private-market setting.

Placing police-oriented individuals in *noncontact,* observe-and-report settings *naturally* creates unreasonably high levels of cognitive dissonance for personnel that often lead to inappropriate behaviors.[9]

Today's Career Environment and its Realities

POLICE ACADEMY GRADUATES

Police academy graduates make up a high percentage of the line personnel in the security industry. Academy graduates are typically young males who don't have

---

[9] See the discussion of SAID in Chapter 4.

actual law enforcement experience but are police trained. They use the security industry as their "pre-career" while waiting for the economy to improve so that police agencies will start hiring. From the academy grads' perspective (and the hiring agency's perspective), working as a security individual provides an excellent opportunity to develop necessary conflict resolution skills. This relationship benefits the academy grad employee and the hiring police agencies, but it might not benefit the private organizations that employ them.

FORMER POLICE OFFICERS

Former police officers make up another significant percentage of private security employment, especially at the senior security management position. Ex-cops are typically older males[10] who have actual law enforcement experience and use the security industry as their second career. These individuals are looking for supplemental income or potential second careers until they retire (again). These relationships benefit the ex-cop/security employee, but they don't always benefit the private organizations that employ them. Both of these police-oriented employee types use the security industry as a placeholder; for police academy graduates it's a stepping-stone, for ex-cops it's their "final resting place."

In fact, the high numbers of police-oriented individuals employed in the private security industry have exacerbated three longstanding security industry myths:

1. Law enforcement training or experience *naturally* prepares individuals for private security employment.
2. There are no other necessary prerequisites or requirements for security employment other than law enforcement training or experience.
3. Security employment is much easier than police work.

VOCATIONAL RELEVANCE

These myths, and the many other unexamined assumptions about the security industry, have led to high levels of vocational irrelevance for today's security personnel. It's unfortunate, but security work is primarily thought of as a job and not a vocation. For many, the vocation was, or will be, a law enforcement career. These ideas are reinforced by the numerous police-oriented personnel who enter the private security industry and consider it a step down and by those who move from the security industry into the law enforcement field and consider it a step up. These industry myths and assumptions interfere with the professionalization process and

---

[10]Women make up a very small percentage of both police and security personnel.

make it much more difficult for security personnel to create vocational relevance; vocational irrelevance interferes with conflict resolution and organizational safety.

No professionalized industry can be successful when a large percentage of its staff continually crosses back and forth between other industries. These trips are a contributing factor for the lack of professional growth in the security industry. It's impossible to create vocational relevance when it relies on other industries for talent.

One of the primary challenges with hiring individuals who are in career holding patterns is that their employment status tends to turn over at a high rate. Academy grads eventually end up getting hired by police departments, and ex-cops often become frustrated by the constraints of the private security market and quit. Constant employment turnover is a deficit in any field and makes it impossible for organizations to create highly productive work environments. The task of maintaining safe organizations requires a cohesive, experienced, productive team of unified personnel who are highly committed to the goals and missions of their organizations and the security departments that employ them. The need to constantly recruit, hire, and train new personnel creates serious financial and productivity costs for organizations. When employees are more focused on their personal circumstances than on the organization's success, these personal circumstances[11] negatively affect employee productivity and organizational safety.

Another benefit of transitioning away from police-oriented personnel and law enforcement community safety philosophies and toward business-minded personnel and organizational safety principles is the opportunity to attract a more diverse workforce. This refocus will naturally create more racial, ethnic, and gender diversity. Diversity has many benefits, and it's generally thought to be a positive attribute of successful organizations (Forbes Insights, 2012). Diversity improves problem solving by involving a multitude of perspectives.

Unfortunately, continuing to emphasize physicality as the primary method for resolving conflict and creating safe organizations keeps the private security industry from becoming more gender and culturally diverse. Deemphasizing physicality and law enforcement training or experience as a prerequisite for employment will also provide more opportunities for women. Women naturally have a difficult time breaking into traditionally male-dominated industries (Kwok, 2010). Since the typical security job description is geared toward male-dominated personality traits, it discourages women from considering a career in the private security industry.

---

[11] Police academy graduates who are in the process of trying to get hired by a police agency often take time off to attend recruitment and testing processes, whereas former police officers often lack the motivation to fully commit to their organizational safety mission because they are financially secure and don't necessarily need to work.

The infusion of more women into the security industry may have a positive impact on conflict resolution. One of the reasons some organizations struggle to effectively resolve conflict is because of an over-reliance on aggressiveness and physicality, in lieu of less intrusive means such as negotiation and collaboration. However, since physical conflict resolution methods may be needed, prospective security personnel, whether male or female, need to be comfortable with the use of physicality as a method for resolving field conflict.[12]

Organizations should recruit security personnel from other internal nonsecurity stakeholder groups and create a robust internal promotional *system* within their own security department to fill security vacancies. Organizations often create unnecessary hiring impediments and expenses for filling their vacant security positions because they haven't developed their own "farm teams." Hiring from within affords several benefits: Applicants understand the social and political nuisances of the organization, there's a much shorter orientation phase, and there is a greater allegiance to the organization's values. By creating an internal promotional system for current employees, security departments can develop internal candidates and alleviate the need to constantly recruit personnel from outside their organizations.

Summary

Resolving conflict in a private setting is *vastly* different from resolving conflict in a public setting. These differences need to be reflected in the types of security personnel that organizations hire. Unfortunately, stakeholders have inadvertently conflated the law enforcement and security environments and their unique and

RECOMMENDATIONS

1. Develop an *in-house* farm team and recruit security personnel candidates from an internal pool of interested organizational stakeholders.

2. Develop key line security personnel to fill promotional openings within the security department.

3. Recruit, hire, train, and retain *business-minded* security personnel, including women and other culturally diverse personnel.

4. De-emphasize police and military experience as a prerequisite for security employment.

---

[12]We are not advocating hiring any individual, regardless of their gender, if they're not able to physically and emotionally deal with the potential for violence associated with conflict resolution.

corresponding community safety philosophies. To improve conflict resolution and organizational safety, organizations need to partner with their security personnel to help them achieve vocational relevance. The most effective way to improve the conflict resolution process is to change the current hiring paradigm from preferring law enforcement-based personnel to preferring more business-minded individuals.

References

Colling, R.L., York, T.W., 2010. Hospital and Healthcare Security (fifth ed.), Boston, MA.

Edley, C.F., Robinson, C.F., 2012. Response to Protests on UC Campuses. Report draft for public comment, 4 May 2012; Web: < http://campusprotestreport.universityofcalifornia.edu > 05.05.12.

Forbes Insights, 2012. Diversity & Inclusion: Unlocking Global Potential Global Diversity Ranking by Country, Sector, and Occupation. n.d.; Web: < www.forbes.com/forbesinsights > 05.07.12.

Kwok, L., 2010. Female entrepreneurs venture into male-dominated industries and thrive. [New Jersey] Star-Ledger, 11 April 2010; Web: < http://blog.nj.com/business > 10.05.12.

Chapter 9

The Role of Training and Trainer Standards

The Problem

Organizations employ security personnel that don't meet professional training standards.

Introduction

Training security personnel creates productive, effective, and efficient employees and provides physical protection for employees and community members while mitigating civil and criminal liabilities. Security personnel need to be trained to responsible and ethical standards. Training standards are necessary for developing effective and responsible security personnel. Responsible training needs to include ethical justifications for the use of protective theories, techniques, tactics, and tools. An effective security training program should provide personnel with a full spectrum of verbal and physical conflict resolution strategies. Trained personnel make better conflict resolution decisions, which improve organizational and community safety and mitigate potential liabilities.

89

Conversely, untrained personnel are liabilities to an organization because they rely on their own conflict resolution values and standards and give very little thought to an organization's priorities. Under stressful interpersonal conflict conditions, untrained personnel will resort to their base instincts. Unfortunately, these instincts range from being overly aggressive with subjects to emotionally disconnecting and being unable to act. Untrained personnel create unsafe conditions for organizational and community members. Paradoxically, senior stakeholders often cite a lack of training in their reluctance to allow security personnel to move beyond observe-and-report-based conflict resolution limits.

Process

Training standards play a major role in organizational safety. It's important for organizations to establish and adopt reliable conflict resolution strategies. Unfortunately, most organizations haven't established a reliable training standard or a systematic training program; they tend to train reactively and haphazardly. Although there are substantive distinctions between the private security industry and the law enforcement industry, the law enforcement community should be emulated for its success in establishing and maintaining effective and universal training standards. Unlike the law enforcement community, the private security industry has failed to create universal and reliable training standards. These failures are partially responsible for negative "security guard" public perceptions and a lack of vocational and organizational relevance.

Potentially Dangerous Encounters (PDEs)

Although it's obvious that police officers have a dangerous job, there are also dangers associated with working in the security field.[1] The Bureau of Labor Statistics (BLS) estimates that over 800,000 municipal police officers are employed throughout the United States.[2] Law enforcement training standards are so effective at creating high levels of officer safety that in spite of being involved in approximately 4 billion potentially dangerous encounters (PDEs) per year, police officers are relatively safe.[3] The BLS also calculates that approximately 1 million security officers

---

[1] We define PDEs as any interpersonal encounter involving immediate physical harm (IPH) or actual physical harm (APH).

[2] This statistic doesn't include all the other types of police work, such as the various federal law enforcement agencies.

[3] Police officer PDEs are calculated based on 10 PDEs per week, per officer. These statistics were calculated based on personnel interviews with local police officers.

are employed in the security industry. These private security officers are involved in approximately 52 million PDEs a year.[4]

According to the 2010 BLS "Fatal Occupational Injuries by Occupations," report, 54 police officers were killed in 2010 during "assault and violent acts," whereas 36 security officers were killed in the same category. We estimate that on average, 1 police officer is killed for every 74 million PDEs, whereas on average 1 security officer is killed for every 1.5 million PDEs.

Based on the quantity and quality of subject interaction, it's not hard to draw two obvious conclusions from this data: First, training makes a substantial contribution to officer safety, and second, security personnel are actually more vulnerable than police officers.

Over the years the national law enforcement community has developed a consistent and unified standard for the use-of-force (or protective action). This professionalized standard is so refined that a police officer can laterally transfer employment from a police department in one part of the country to a police department in another part of the country and notice only minor use-of-force policy differences. Unlike the law enforcement industry, the private security industry's use-of-force standard often differs from organization to organization—and sometimes from moment to moment.[5]

The lack of a professionalized security standard, along with these training and policy inconsistencies, is in part due to the competitive nature of the private market. However, an overemphasis on risk aversion policies, the misapplication of public law enforcement philosophies to private organizations, and the preference for observe-and-report organizational safety philosophies are other substantial impediments to standardization.

Philosophical Approaches to Training

There are two distinct philosophical approaches typically used for training private security personnel: enforcement or protection. The enforcement- and protection-based training philosophies are mutually exclusive and incompatible; enforcement is a reactive strategy, whereas protection is proactive.

---

[4] Security officer PDEs are calculated based on 1 PDEs per week, per officer. Although these statistics are subjective they are calculated based on personal experience, personnel interviews, and opinion surveys conducted with local security officers.

[5] In reaction to the UC Davis pepper-spray incident in October 2011, one of my clients suggested removing pepper spray from their security personnel's protective duty gear array. The client justified leaving their security personnel "defenseless" based on "possible" negative public perceptions associated with the use of pepper spray. They made a conscious choice that protecting their reputation had a greater value than protecting their security personnel or community members.

Protection-based training is preferred because it supports an organization's primary organizational safety mission of providing high levels of safety for both community members and employees. Protection-based training is easily integrated into an organization's basic business operating systems and supports an ORAP organizational safety model.[6] Unlike protective-based training, enforcement-based training functions best in a public law enforcement context and relies on statutory authority[7] that private security personnel don't possess.

Enforcement plays an important role in creating safe public environments, but when used by private security personnel, it's counterproductive and ineffective.

Over the years the security industry has failed to create its own private market approach to training and instead has relied on law enforcement (or law enforcement lite) training. Unfortunately, these experiments have created confusion in the security industry and within organizations that employ security personnel. Trainers continue to waste time either editing law enforcement training to meet their needs or issuing disclaimers when utilizing law enforcement training.[8]

Training plays an important role in conflict resolution and mitigating potential liability.[9] Without training, it's impossible to determine how perfectly obedient security personnel will act when faced with a violent individual. Will they freeze and fail to defend themselves and suffer serious injuries, such as mental, emotional, or physical damage, or need to file a worker's compensation claim? Or will they snap and overreact and beat an uncooperative suspect into a coma, creating tort claims for millions of dollars? Training security personnel in protective theories, tactics, and tools helps create responsible personnel and safe organizations.

Organizations that fail to adequately train personnel open themselves up to negligent training lawsuits. These are some of the most difficult and costly lawsuits for organizations to defend.[10] Community members, including legal and civil institutions, have high expectations for adequately trained personnel in all job categories. However, because of the unique nature of a security individual's job task, which includes the possibility of confronting violent individuals and carrying protective tools or devices, institutions of accountability tend to hold security personnel to high training standards.

---

[6] See Chapter 3 for a more detailed exposition of ORAP and the OSA mode.

[7] Statutory authority is discussed later in this chapter.

[8] These private-market training challenges were the impetus for the creation of the Force Decisions Institute.

[9] Specific training theories and tactics are covered in more detail in Chapters 9, 10, and 11.

[10] Although *Canton v. Harris* (1989) involves a failure to train police officers, the underlying legal concept is well established in tort law and relates to private entities. The two basic vulnerabilities are: (1) a lack of training in an area where there's a patently obvious need for training, and (2) an established pattern of conduct by personnel that would put the final policymaker on notice and the policymaker failed to respond to it with adequate training and policies.

For example, in the case of Weaver v. Event Staffing, et al., claimant Daniel Weaver sued Event Staffing, a security company, and its security personnel, alleging they were responsible for Weaver's physical injuries that left him a quadriplegic. The lawsuit claims that Event Staffing "failed to properly train" its employees, which led to Weaver's injuries (Associated Press, "Man sues over paralyzing injury at West VA event"). This is only one of the thousands of claims[11] made each year against security personnel and organizations that aren't adequately trained for the challenges of private-market conflict resolution.

Unfortunately, some short-sighted stakeholders continue to minimize or completely dismiss the importance and value of security personnel training. There are several reasons often cited for these failures to adequately train personnel: indirect budgetary control, noncontact or overly restrictive use-of-force policies, and stakeholder bias.

Noncontact or overly restrictive use-of-force policies are responsible for many of the challenges found in the security industry. Unfortunately, these conflict resolution approaches may create an impression among some stakeholders that security personnel don't need training because their policy prohibits personnel from getting involved. I've been asked many times by senior stakeholders, "How much training does it really take to observe and report and stay out of trouble?" This question represents a flawed view of organizational safety from any perspective. Even if stakeholders honestly believed that noncontact or restrictive use-of-force policies were the best option for their organizations, security personnel would still need to be trained in physical conflict avoidance. In reality, organizations have limited control over their security personnel actions and no control over the behaviors of the dangerous subjects with which they regularly come into contact.

Funding

Although training is not really an option for some organizations, funding the training program is. Senior organizational stakeholders often don't provide security departments the necessary training funds to support their security personnel. Unfortunately, some organizations still don't allocate necessary funds to support reliable security training programs.[12] From a business perspective, it's much easier

---

[11] Unlike public sector lawsuits, it's much more difficult to determine the details of current private-market negligent lawsuits because the vast majority of settlements involve parties that have entered into confidentiality agreements. This unique private-market litigation constraint continues to exacerbate two historic risk management myths: One, senior nonsecurity stakeholders often exaggerate the risks associated with physical intervention, and two, security personnel often use it to minimize the risk.

[12] The absence of reliable training standards is an impediment to funding. It's impossible to determine the training costs without first determining what specific training should be required, preferred, or desired.

to justify spending money in departments that generate income. However, responsible organizations also know the general business axiom of spending money in the here and now, to prevent or reduce future expenses and liabilities. Since security departments don't typically generate income for their organizations, as some other departments do, security-related spending is often a point of contention during budget discussions. Unfortunately, during tough economic times, organizations often look to cut spending in nonrevenue-generating departments, and security-related expenses are often the first casualties.

Since training is a cost and the savings are not always immediately noticed, it's difficult for some stakeholders to justify personnel training expenses. It's also difficult to quantify the savings derived from personnel training, making it even more difficult to justify the spending.[13] To educate senior stakeholders on the importance of training, senior security managers need to become experts at quantifying the many benefits of employing professionally trained security personnel.

Although it's difficult to quantify the exact dollar amount that's saved by training personnel, it's easy to determine the costs associated with a negligence lawsuit for failing to train. Training is an excellent investment and has a quantifiable business return on investment. Budget-based risk management is short sighted and ultimately leads to decreases in organizational safety and increases in potential liabilities.

Finally, some stakeholders still falsely believe that training actually makes security personnel more likely to act inappropriately or to behave criminally when faced with stressful interpersonal field conflict. Paradoxically, these same stakeholders believe that other types of personnel training or certifications play a valuable role in terms of safety.[14] Unfortunately for these stakeholders and for the organizations that employ them, it often takes a serious event, such as an major injury to a customer, employee, or security individual, to focus an organization's attention on the importance of training. It's been long established that personnel training plays an important role in every industry and in every unique job classification; security training is no exception.

Qualities of Effective Standards

RELIABILITY

Establishing reliable security personnel training standards is the first step in preparing personnel for the mission of resolving field conflict and maintaining safe

---

[13] Since security spending is often made by nonsecurity stakeholders who are situated much higher in the organizational and social-political structure than the senior security manager, it's often difficult for senior stakeholders to completely understand the security department's training needs.

[14] There are many types of business training, including required continuing education and mechanical certifications, e.g., forklift training, blood-borne pathogens, and so on.

organizations. Since it's impossible for security personnel to avoid conflict, training should include both verbal *and* physical conflict resolution strategies.

As a security consultant and trainer, one of the questions I'm most often asked is, "What exactly should my security personnel be trained in?" Unlike other professionalized industries that have established national training standards, the security industry has yet to create one. A lack of a national training standard is an additional impediment to convincing senior stakeholders to provide security departments with responsible training budgets.

Charles P. Nemeth, a recognized security expert, argues that the security industry will be held to its own professional (or nonprofessional) standards. Nemeth writes, "What is certain is that the security industry will be held to its own standard of professional conduct and that injuries that result will be scrutinized in accordance with our expectations of performance and due care owed" (Nemeth, 2005 p. 136). In other words, negative field conflict outcomes will be evaluated based on the standards we create or fail to create.

The selection of recommended personnel training and duty equipment (tools or devices) should be the result of a thorough security task and process assessment, integrated with a detailed risk and vulnerability assessment. These assessments provide the basis for determining the proper level of personnel training and for the selection of duty gear for each unique operating context. For example, a firearm may be an appropriate tool for resolving conflict in some contexts, but in other private settings it may be a liability.

APPLICABILITY

Regardless of the context or the perceived organizational safety threat, all professional security personnel need to be trained in both business and organizational safety principles. Training in business principles protects the employer; training in organizational safety principles protects personnel and potential crime victims. The *minimum* security personnel training standard should include these areas:

1. Training in business-focused principles (e.g., supply and demand, profit and loss, and risk management)
2. A thorough orientation on the processes involved in selling or providing an organization's specific product or service to their unique market (e.g., universities, hospitals, or retail)
3. Security and safety training in protective theories, techniques, tactics, and tools

Having a thorough understanding of basic business principles, such as how an organization's unique product or service is sold or provided to its unique market and how security individuals' specific activities provide value for their organization, maximizes security personnel effectiveness.

Unfortunately, too many security personnel don't have a clue as to how their activities create relevance for their organizations. This is one of the missing links in security personnel training. For training to be useful, personnel need to understand how the theories, techniques, tactics, and tools they train in provide relevance, not only for themselves but for their organizations. This ignorance continues to be one of the weaknesses of the security industry and an impediment to attaining professionalism.

BASIC TRAINING

The minimum private security personnel training standard should include three mandated courses of instruction: verbal tactics, weaponless protective measures,[15] and the Situational Protective Action Risk Continuum or SPARC use-of-force training. Since the vast majority of private security personnel don't carry protective or defensive tools or devices and they're employed in environments where they can't avoid being confronted by uncooperative subjects, they need reliable and ethical ways to protect themselves and others. It's irresponsible for any organization or security department to assign security personnel in the field without this basic training. These three courses of instruction are the *minimum* required training for all security personnel in all contexts.[16]

Verbal tactics training teaches security personnel how to use verbal communication as an effective tool for negotiating subject cooperation and for resolving interpersonal field conflict.[17] When verbal communication fails and protective action becomes necessary, weaponless protective measures provide security personnel a reliable method to protect themselves and others against unarmed physical assaults, without the need to use defensive weapons (e.g., baton, OC/pepper spray, or Taser). SPARC use-of-force training outlines the proper context for the use of an organization's approved conflict resolution options.

Verbal tactics, weaponless protective measures, and SPARC use-of-force training are the foundational building blocks of effective field conflict resolution strategies.

Depending on the complexities of the unique employment environment, security personnel may require additional training in other protective theories, techniques, tactics, and tools.

CONTENT RICH

Effective and reliable personnel training needs to include four important learning components:

1. Judgment
2. Justification

---

[15] Traditionally, "hand-to-hand" training is called weaponless self-defense, or WSD. However, in our protective philosophy we call it weaponless protective measures, or WPM.

[16] This training standard is over and above any statutory or regulatory mandated security personnel training.

[17] We've created a proprietary verbal tactics system called DEACONS, as detailed in Chapter 11.

3. Mechanics
4. Competency testing

Judgment

Judgment comes into play when it's appropriate to act (or to refrain from acting).

Since judgment is hard to teach, it's rarely a component of personnel training. Judgment training involves creating circumstances that are as "real" as possible compared to actual interactions that security personnel would find themselves in and then evaluating how personnel respond when confronted with those circumstances. Judgment is typically taught through role-playing exercises. However, good role-playing exercises are time consuming to set up, involve the coordination of many people, and are not multicontextual. Video simulation is a much better option for teaching security personnel judgment skills.[18]

Justification

The *rationale* for choosing and using a specific protective tactic, tool, device, or weapon in a given context.

Justification needs to fit into an organization's overall basic business operating philosophy. Justification for choosing and using a certain tactic or tool is typically taught through an approved use-of-force matrix that provides security personnel with their various protective action options.[19]

Mechanics

Mechanics involve how to use or apply a tactic, tool, device, or weapon.

Mechanical competency is the easiest of these learning components to teach. In a nonstress training environment, virtually anyone can be taught how to use the type of tactics, tools, devices, or weapons that are generally used by security personnel. Mechanics is taught through theory building and hands-on instruction.

Unfortunately, the majority of industry-wide security personnel training focuses exclusively on the mechanical component of learning while virtually ignoring the importance of instruction in judgment and justification.

---

[18] We recommend Golden, CO. based TI Training's interactive scenario training (IST) program (www.titraining.com). IST plays an important role in improving verbal tactics competency. IST provides students a safe and realistic environment to practice their verbal tactics skills in a realistic setting *prior* to using them in actual field encounters. Verbal tactics competency is enhanced through the use of live role-playing and video interactive conflict scenarios.

[19] See the Force Decisions Institute's SPARC chart in Chapter 11.

Competency Testing

Theoretical and mechanical competency testing is an important but rarely used component of a reliable security training program. Personnel need to be tested using both written and hands-on proficiency exams to ensure that personnel meet the minimum competency levels for each course of instruction. There's very little value in personnel training that's not validated for competency. Unfortunately, many security training courses are created with no way to fail! For a training standard to be reliable (and useful), there has to be both a minimum competency level and a level of performance that fails to meet the standard.

ONGOING AND CONTINUOUS TRAINING

In addition to the four listed learning components of reliable training, training needs to be ongoing and continuous. Training skills are perishable; the theories, techniques, and tactics initially learned naturally degrade overtime if not practiced. Ongoing training also ensures that personnel become familiar with new laws, theories, and techniques while also communicating the organization's commitment to the professionalization process.

If tactical or mechanical skills are not regularly practiced, renewed, and retrained, they become less effective over time and could become a potential liability for personnel and their organizations if they're improperly applied in field use and a claim of inappropriate force is made. Therefore, an effective training program also needs to be supported by ongoing and continuous personnel training. Organizations need to establish a list of security or safety theories, practices, and tactics that should be refreshed or renewed yearly or biyearly.[20]

REALISM

Effective security training needs to be as realistic as possible. Even in organizations that prohibit or restrict subject contact, security personnel still need to learn how to protect themselves from violent individuals. Unfortunately, most security training is theory based and unrealistic. Although theory only training is easier to teach, less expensive, and no one gets hurt, it's ineffective.[21] The wide range of acceptable security officer physical fitness levels in the private security industry is an impediment to the creation of serious personnel training standards.[22]

---

[20] We recommend that security personnel receive yearly refresher training for any tool or device that they carry.

[21] No reliable training standard can guarantee injury-free training. However, injuries suffered during training are more controllable, are less severe, and create much less liability than injuries suffered during an actual field conflict by unfit, obese and unprepared security personnel.

[22] Physically unfit personnel or obese are much more likely to be injured during attempts to resolve conflict than are physically fit personnel. See a study by Dr. Alexander Eastman on police officer injuries, reported in the *Force Science Institute* #207; www.forcescience.org.

Unlike the military and many law enforcement agencies that have strict physical fitness standards and place a high value on physical fitness and wellness, the private security industry has refused to embrace this as a core value.[23] The private security industry and the organizations that employ security personnel have been reluctant to require a physical fitness standard for private security personnel.

The reluctance to require a physical fitness standard impedes the professionalization process. Since perception plays a major role in personnel and corporate safety and task effectiveness, being unfit or obese contributes to the already stable negative cultural perceptions of the "overweight and inept" security guard. Practically speaking, it's impossible to protect someone when the protectors are a danger to themselves!

These security personnel physical limitations make it impossible to create rigorous and realistic training standards. The absence of a physically fit security personnel is also used by organizations to justify "hands-off" subject contact policies and their preference for observe-and-report organizational safety models.

Paradoxically, even organizations that require (or suggest), as a condition of employment or as a condition of continued employment, that security personnel use physical conflict resolution strategies to maintain safe environments don't have a physical fitness standard. However, to maintain safe organizations, protect community members, and minimize workplace violence, security personnel need to be held to a reliable physical fitness standard and receive practical and realistic training. Unfit and obese security personnel are unable to "protect and serve" and are a serious liability for organizations.[24]

TRAINER STANDARDS

Perhaps one of the most controversial areas of private security training (and one that's rarely discussed) is security trainer qualifications. Historically, the assumption has always been that current or former police officers make the best security trainers However, this is another example of the many unexamined security industry assumptions that have become naturalized over the years.

For security personnel to meet their protective mission, they need to be trained to a nonlaw enforcement training standard and taught by qualified instructors that understand the unique challenges of providing security services to free-market

---

[23] The UC Irvine, California, Medical Center Security Department is one exception. In January 2013, they implemented a comprehensive physical fitness standard for their security officers.

[24] Unfortunately, many organizations falsely believe they can't require a physical fitness standard for security personnel unless it's applied equally to *all* organizational members. In other words, if a fitness standard is implemented, it must apply equally to all employees, including nonsecurity personnel. Several of our security clients have made a successful transition to a serious physical fitness standard.

organizations. The substantive differences between the law enforcement and private security industries make it untenable to create one training standard that meets the needs of both industries. In fact, attempts to create a single standard have created a confused private security training standard that has resulted in decreases in safety and increases in potential liability.

Unfortunately, these unexamined training assumptions can have a devastating impact on private organizations. Often, senior stakeholders are unaware of their senior security managers' training decisions. The decision to use law enforcement trainers is further complicated because many senior security managers are themselves former police officers or have a natural affinity for law enforcement personnel. These personal preferences may be the impetus for preferring law enforcement training and law enforcement trainers over uniquely private-market solutions. In the end, these training preferences may create unintended consequences for private security personnel and their organizations.

CONTEXT, TRAINING, AND TRAINERS

Although these two industries operate under very different legal, philosophical, and cultural principles, many decision makers, both security and nonsecurity stakeholders, continue to conflate these two industries based on their superficial similarities (e.g., wearing similar-looking uniforms, carrying police equipment, or interacting with criminal behavior). Law enforcement tactics and defensive tools are applied in a unique public context where police officers have statutory authority, scope of employment immunity, extensive training (up to 1,000 hours prior to working in the field, supervised field training, and ongoing and continuous post-employment training), and high levels of community support. Unlike police officers, security personnel employed by private organizations have none of these advantages. In fact, in the private sector, if a private security individual takes action (or if he or she decides not to act), the individual and the employer could be sued, even if the individual's actions were *both* legal and ethical.

LAW ENFORCEMENT TRAINERS

Although many law enforcement trainers are experts in the use of certain defensive tools (e.g., firearms, baton, OC/pepper spray, or Taser) and tactics (such as weaponless self-defense) and are skilled instructors, they're not experts in the application of these theories or tactics in an non-sworn, private context. Law enforcement officers don't have actual experience using these theories, tactics, or tools in an non-sworn, free-market, private security environment. In the training community, a lack of actual experience is widely perceived as a liability. Law enforcement trainers may be experts at how to use certain defensive tools or tactics, but they're not experts on knowing *when* to apply them in a private security context.

This fact should not be ignored or minimized: Not knowing when it's appropriate to apply force exposes private organizations to unnecessary liability.

Not having experience applying defensive tools or tactics in a unique and distinctive private context, coupled with a generalized lack of understanding of free-market principles, may increase liability for organizations that utilize law enforcement trainers. In fact, law enforcement trainers who train private security personnel create additional areas of vulnerability for private organizations, such as being drawn into a training lawsuit involving private security personnel they've trained. How would a law enforcement officer testify in court to his/her own personnel experience using the theories, tools, and tactics he/she teaches when he's/she's never actually applied them while employed as a private uniformed security individual?

TRAINER QUALIFICATIONS

This training rationale is not new to law enforcement trainers or to law enforcement training. It happens to be the same reasoning that law enforcement personnel use to disqualify civilian security trainers from training law enforcement officers. In the law enforcement industry, private (non-sworn) trainers are rarely accepted as qualified law enforcement instructors.[25] In fact, the POST[26] training standard is so strong that under some circumstances it even prohibits former or retired police officers from instructing active-duty police officers.[27] To be a POST-approved instructor, the instructor has to be an active-duty police officer, and the curriculum and the facility has to be POST-approved. The law enforcement community has very high standards for both the individuals they accept as qualified to teach and for their approved training curriculum.

Serious training standards are responsible for high levels of peace officer safety and minimized potential liability.

Paradoxically, most law enforcement trainers don't think POST's methodology and reasoning for qualifying law enforcement trainers should be used to qualify private security trainers. The overwhelming majority of law enforcement officers, security managers, and senior stakeholders assume that active, former, or retired law enforcement officers make the best security trainers. For some unexplained reason, law enforcement trainers believe that law enforcement experience is necessary for training law enforcement officers, but actual security experience is not necessary for training security personnel. These inconsistent training theories are impediments to the creation of unique private security industry training standards.

---

[25] There are some exceptions to this general rule, such as civilian instructors who have law enforcement or military experience, and/or if they're teaching a specialized training course that's in high demand and not generally taught by the law enforcement community.

[26] POST is a universal acronym for Peace Officer Standards and Training. Every state has a POST entity that ensures police officer standards.

[27] This is the California POST training standard.

The private security industry should create a professional standard for qualifying individuals who are certified to train private security personnel and create a unique nonenforcement certified training curriculum instead of relying on the law enforcement industry. Even though it may seem counterintuitive, relying on law enforcement personnel to set the training standard impedes the security industry's professionalization process. Although we don't recommend using a POST training curriculum, we do recommend that the private security industry adopt training principles similar to POST, such as requiring actual private security work experience, the use of certified training courses, and mastery of free-market particulars, including a strong foundation for business principles, intellectual vitality, and dedication to the security vocation.

LAW ENFORCEMENT TRAINING CHALLENGES

There are several problems associated with teaching private security personnel law enforcement theories, techniques, tactics, or tools. The primary problem is that it demonstrates a lack of understanding of the enabling role that statutory authority and scope of employment immunity play in the activation of law enforcement training effectiveness. Statutory authority creates a legal obligation for citizens to cooperate with the police, whereas scope of employment immunity protects police officers and their employing agencies against many types of civil and criminal liabilities. Unlike police officers, private security personnel can't take advantage of the "activating power" of statutory authority or scope of employment immunity in attempting to resolve private-market interpersonal field conflict.

Almost every private organization, especially those organizations that employ their own proprietary (in-house) security personnel, hires police-oriented personnel (academy graduates and former or retired police officers). In fact, many of these police-oriented individuals have extensive police experience and POST training. However, once these former law enforcement officers "suit up" as non-sworn, private, uniformed security personnel, they lose a great deal of influence over uncooperative subjects because they no longer have access to statutory authority or scope of employment immunity.

It's been well established that the *effectiveness* of law enforcement training is primarily the result of statutory authority and scope of employment immunity, *not* of the specific individual's character, training, pay, or the tools he or she carries.

Law enforcement training also confuses private security personnel by minimizing and conflating (directly or indirectly) the substantive principal differences between these two industries. This confusion is further exacerbated, since many security personnel are former law enforcement officers, which makes them more susceptible to social-psychological police influences such as mimicking law enforcement behavior or preferring law enforcement conflict resolution tactics over uniquely private-market methods.

Training private security personnel in law enforcement techniques, tactics, or tools increases potential civil and criminal liability. Private security personnel operate as agents of the owners of the property to which they're assigned. Unlike police officers, private security personnel have narrow physical interaction limits for resolving field conflict. Under most circumstances, organizations don't want their security personnel using hands-on force to resolve conflict. (In extreme cases, security personnel are prohibited from using force, even when it may help protect their own lives.) Unlike security training, law enforcement training emphasizes enforcement and the use of physical force to resolve conflict.

Summary

To create safe and secure organizations, organizations need professionally trained security personnel who are trained to an effective and professional private security training standard. Organizations should use qualified trainers who understand the unique challenges of providing security services to the free market. Trained security personnel make better conflict resolution decisions, create higher levels of personal and organizational safety, and mitigate potential liability.

RECOMMENDATIONS

1. Establish a responsible training budget.
2. Create reliable training standards, including minimum yearly training hours.
3. Train security personnel in a full spectrum of conflict resolution strategies.
4. Use realistic training theories and tactics.
5. Establish appropriate duty gear or protective tool array.
6. Create and maintain reliable physical fitness standards.
7. Create and maintain security trainer standards and qualifications.

References

"NY man sues over paralyzing injury at W. VA. event." Associated Press, In: Wall Street Journal. 17 May 2012; Web: http://online.wsj.com/article/APb83daae0af2c4a96a52b2800dbcdd888, 7 June 2012.

Nemeth, C.P., 2005. Private Security and the Law, third ed., Boston, MA.

Implementing Conflict Resolution Strategies

Verbal Conflict Resolution Strategies: Theories, Techniques, and Tactics for Resolving Conflict

The Problem

Security personnel aren't adequately trained in the proper use of verbal conflict resolution strategies.

Introduction

Successful conflict resolution depends on competent communicators. Verbal strategies for resolving conflict are the most important protective theories, techniques, and tactics available to security personnel. Since most field conflict can be resolved verbally, without the need to use physical force, security personnel need to become competent in the use of verbal conflict resolution strategies.

Verbal strategies are nonphysical contact conflict resolution techniques and tactics.[1] Although security personnel should develop competency in verbal strategies,

---

[1] We don't consider verbal tactics force.

in rare circumstances when verbal strategies aren't effective, personnel need to use physical conflict resolution strategies.[2]

Process

Effective verbal conflict resolution tactics include verbal de-escalation, perceptions of personnel effectiveness, command presence, dialogue, and verbal commands. A recent University of California (UC) report supports the contention that verbal skills training is an imperative for personnel who interact with uncooperative individuals. Their report highlighted a lack of verbal skills training by their police officers as a contributing factor for a recent campus protest turning violent.

In a report written by UC Dean Christopher F. Edley, Jr., and UC General Counsel Charles F. Robinson in response to an allegation of excessive force on the part of UC Davis police officers, the writers concluded that UC police officers lacked training in verbal de-escalation techniques and made a recommendation that the UC system should only hire police officers who have the right temperament to deal with "taunting and other disrespectful behavior … without resorting to physical force" (Edley and Robinson, 2012 pp. 49 and 62).

Perspectives on the Effectiveness of Verbal Strategies

Nonsecurity stakeholders and security personnel have differing opinions on the role and effectiveness of verbal conflict resolution strategies. Unfortunately, both security personnel and nonsecurity stakeholders make critical communication assumptions. Nonsecurity stakeholders typically overestimate communication's effectiveness, whereas security personnel usually underestimate communication's value. Security personnel tend to move too quickly through the communication process and fast-forward to the use of physical strategies to resolve conflict. On the other hand, nonsecurity stakeholders generally assume that if conflict escalates to violence and security personnel are involved, it's probably because they failed to properly use communication.

Both security and nonsecurity stakeholders agree that the majority of interpersonal field conflict can be resolved with proper communication techniques. However, security personnel are still more skeptical than nonsecurity stakeholders that communication solutions will generally lead to an effective resolution. Unfortunately, these communication assumptions may create the unintended consequence of decreases in organizational and community safety and increases in potential liability.

---

[2] See Chapter 11 for a detailed exposition of physical conflict strategies.

In an effort to minimize potential civil liability, many organizations have enacted noncontact or overly restrictive use-of-force policies that emphasize communication as the best, and perhaps only, authorized strategy for resolving field conflict. This noncontact approach to interpersonal conflict has the potential to create a false sense of security for personnel when they're dealing with aggressive individuals. In reality, not all field conflict can be peacefully resolved, and physical conflict resolution strategies are needed when communicative solutions fail.

Police officers are partially responsible for the misperception that *talk* is the most effective technique for conflict resolution.[3] Police officers are trained in various communication tactics, including a communication system called Verbal Judo.® It's true that mastering various communication techniques will increase the possibility that uncooperative individuals will peacefully submit; however, it's not the primary reason these techniques work. Police officer training effectiveness is primarily the result of officers' legal or statutory authority, not because of perfectly applied techniques.[4] The individual police officer applying these verbal techniques knows (and so do uncooperative subjects) that at the end of the verbal interaction, if the uncooperative subject still refuses to cooperate with the police officer, the subject has committed a criminal act and could be arrested.[5] Unlike police officer interactions, private security personnel know (and so do uncooperative subjects) that resisting a private security individual is not a crime. A lack of statutory authority creates a distinct disadvantage for private security personnel. Although it's true that these public/private distinctions make a difference in a technique's effectiveness, verbal skills play an important role in successful interpersonal field conflict resolution.

It's unfortunate, but some senior security personnel still believe that private security personnel should receive instruction in enforcement-based POST training,[6] even though private personnel don't possess the requisite statutory authority necessary to enable law enforcement training. Since POST training is reliable, systematized, and inexpensive,[7] it's easy to understand why security managers would want to use it. This isn't true of private security training.

However, the failure of senior private security managers to understand the enabling role that statutory authority plays in creating law enforcement training effectiveness

---

[3]Compared to the high quantity of PDEs in which they're involved, their verbal skills seem to be extremely effective at creating safe interactions.

[4]Even given these limitations, verbal tactics training is one of the most important skills security personnel should possess.

[5]See California Penal Codes 148, 834 (a), 836.6 (a) and (b), et al.

[6]California PC 832 training is one example.

[7]No matter how well it's presented or how inexpensive it is, law enforcement training is not appropriate for private personnel. These "savings" will end up costing organizations much more in future liabilities for the misapplication of law enforcement tactics in a private setting.

has led to an enormous waste of time, resources, and finances for many private organizations.

In fact, training private security personnel in law enforcement tactics confuses personnel and exacerbates the tendency for security personnel to emphasize physical conflict resolution strategies[8] over less intrusive and more collaborative solutions, creating unnecessary civil liability.

The key to resolving interpersonal conflict is gaining the involved subject's cooperation early in the conflict behavioral phase.[9] There are only two methods for gaining a subject's cooperation: Create an environment where the subject is likely to voluntarily cooperate, or use physical conflict strategies to force compliance. When faced with field conflict, security personnel should try to verbally convince subjects that it's in their best interests to cooperate with them. However, when subjects are in a heightened emotional state, under the influence of drugs and/or alcohol, or in mental or emotional distress, this is an extremely complicated task. Many uncooperative subjects are not easily convinced of what's in their best interests during times of intoxication or emotional stress. Often, initially passive aggressive subjects become physically aggressive with security personnel. Effective verbal skills can help personnel better resolve conflict and *reduce* (not eliminate) the need to use force or protective action.

The Ability to Influence

Social power plays an important role in resolving interpersonal field conflict, especially in interacting with uncooperative, dangerous, or violent subjects. Since private security personnel don't enjoy statutory authority and since most organizations severely limit their security personnel's authority, personnel need to utilize social power along with communication to improve organizational safety.

Kathy Henning, 2012 identifies five power types that influence the conflict resolution process:

1. *Legitimate* power is being hired, elected, or appointed to a powerful position.
2. *Referent* power is being liked.
3. *Coercive* power is the ability to punish.
4. *Reward* power is the ability to reward.
5. *Expert* power is knowledge or experience.

According to Henning, one of the keys to effective conflict resolution is determining which party has the greater *power level* and then creating conflict resolution strategies based on those power *inequities*.

---

[8] See Chapter 4 for a detailed exposition of the negative aspects of SAID.

[9] The conflict behavioral phases are passive-aggressive, direct aggression, and active violence.

Although Henning lists five power types, we've expanded the power list to seven by rounding out the list with two additional types:

6. *Physical* power is the *visually* obvious physical advantage a security individual has over his adversary, such as height, weight, and muscular build.
7. *Ethical/moral* powers are *universal* community values embodied by the majority of community members that align with the security individual's values.

Individuals involved in the conflict resolution process may embody and demonstrate power, deliberately withhold power, or exercise more than one of these power types simultaneously during attempts to resolve conflict. For instance, a parent may be able to physically discipline (coercive) her child or reward the child with ice cream—two power types to overcome her child's resistance to cleaning his room. However, unlike the frustrations associated with trying to get a child to clean his room, frustrations associated with attempting to resolve field conflict *without* understanding the role that social power plays may create power *imbalances* that lead to unsafe, violent, or even deadly consequences for security personnel.

Since most private security personnel are not typically afforded high levels of *legitimate* power by their organizations, they need to rely on *referent, expert, physical, or ethical/moral* power to successfully resolve interpersonal field conflict.

Verbal Tactics

To effectively resolve interpersonal conflict, security personnel need to become competent in verbal tactics. Conversely, ineffective communication skills may be responsible for exacerbating and, under some conditions, instigating and escalating field conflict. Effective communication improves security personnel's chances of creating an environment in which subject cooperation is likely to occur. If attempts to negotiate subject cooperation fail and the interaction involves potential or active physical harm, it may be appropriate to resort to physical conflict resolution strategies to protect individuals. Physical protective strategies should only be utilized after attempts to negotiate subject cooperation fail or if they're an inappropriate option for the given circumstance.

Verbal tactics are defined as communication skills used by personnel when talking to uncooperative subjects for the purpose of negotiating subject cooperation and for reducing the need to use physical conflict resolution strategies.

Personnel who master verbal tactics are typically involved in fewer physical confrontations. Since the majority of security personnel's injuries are the result of physical confrontations with aggressive subjects, the application of verbal tactics has the potential to *greatly* reduce employee, personnel, and subject injuries as well as workers compensation and negligence claims. When faced with conflict, security personnel's primary goal is to gain control of a situation or over a subject with the least amount of physical influence as possible. Verbal tactics are most effective when used in conjunction with security personnel command presence.

Negotiating Subject Cooperation

Negotiating subject cooperation is defined as a systematic communicative process that aims to create a productive environment whereby initially resistant subjects will choose to cooperate with security personnel.

When security personnel are able to successfully negotiate subject cooperation and don't need to use protective action to gain cooperation, personnel and organizational safety improve and potential civil and criminal liability is mitigated.

Verbal Tactics: How To

The following are the primary verbal tactics used to negotiate subject cooperation.

1. Command Presence
2. Dialogue
3. Verbal commands

Even though security personnel command presence is not technically a verbal strategy, it's included in verbal tactics because it's an ancillary and related component of an effective verbal message. Command presence functions alongside the verbal message to reinforce or support it. Command presence communicates messages through nonlinguistic means or through the use of body language.

Security personnel command presence is a core nonverbal communication tactic that aids in the negotiating subject cooperation process. Security personnel command presence is created through the synthesis of body language, physical appearance, and tone of voice. Communication studies show that nonverbal communication, also known as *body language*, communicates powerful messages alongside the spoken message. It's often argued that more is communicated through body language than through the spoken word. To be effective, security personnel need to be aware that their body language and their physical appearance "communicate without words."

Security personnel command presence is defined as the social-psychological influence created through verbal communication, tone of voice, body language, and physical appearance, which influences some people under certain conditions and at certain times.

Command presence is an important component of negotiating subject cooperation; however, it is temporary, fleeting, and ultimately unsustainable over time.

Under some circumstances, it may not take long for a subject to figure out that security personnel have little or no real authority or power, creating a power struggle between security personnel and resistant subjects, whereas under other conditions initially resistant subjects will fully submit to the security personnel's verbal instruction. Security personnel need to be cautious in attempting to assert themselves into highly emotional circumstances, because power struggles can quickly escalate into violent interactions. Once power shifts from security personnel to uncooperative subjects, security personnel have a limited timeframe in which to apply a verbal strategy before they become ineffective and physical force is necessary to control the situation.

The *power of presence* is created through a combination of the security personnel's verbal and physical attributes and a community's socialized response for interacting with perceived authority figures in a given context. Initially when personnel exert command presence, conflict may temporarily escalate until social power is balanced. However, once security personnel establish effective command presence, there's a greater likelihood that their influence will affect behavior. When security personnel use their verbal skills to de-escalate conflict, they're better able to resolve conflict using lower levels of physical force.

Security personnel's appearance plays an important role in the conflict resolution process.[10] Although a security employee's look or how she is perceived is not verbal communication, it does play an important role in how her verbal communication is interpreted. Being perceived as a professional could be a deterrent to some uncooperative or potentially assaultive individuals. Potentially uncooperative subjects will often "size up" or test a security individual's ability to professionally perform her job based solely on how she is perceived. Hardened criminals may decide in a matter of seconds whether they perceive security personnel to be worthy adversaries. Therefore, even the perception that security personnel are in charge during a field conflict plays a role in fending off a potential physical assault.

A security individual's tone of voice can communicate control or weakness during attempts to resolve interpersonal field conflict. It's important for security personnel to maintain emotional control of their tone of voice, especially under stressful circumstances. The majority of content listeners actually hear is communicated through the way the message is delivered.

The verbal characteristics of tone of voice are:

1. *Pace.* The speed at which one speaks.
2. *Modulation.* The rhythm of one's spoken word.
3. *Pitch.* How high or low one's voice sounds.
4. *Volume.* How soft or loud one speaks.

---

[10] See Chapter 4 for a more detailed exposition of the role of uniforms.

Verbal Commands

Verbal commands are defined as a formal and authoritative-sounding form of communication used with a serious tone and an increase in volume and intensity, applied with the goal of convincing subjects to immediately stop or start some preferred behavior.

If the pace of field conflict allows for it and if it's appropriate, security personnel should give strong verbal warnings to an uncooperative subject *prior* to the application of protective techniques, tactics, or tools and/or *during* their application.[11] Security personnel need to be perceived as in control of the conflict without being perceived as being punitive. Verbal commands should be used simultaneously and in concert with the application of protective tactics.

Since most people are passionate about their rights and the freedom to express themselves, they naturally don't like being told what to do by authority figures, so security personnel need to be prepared for resistance. These interactions are further complicated when the authority figure is perceived as having little or no authority, which is true of most private security personnel. To optimize their success for negotiating subject cooperation, security personnel need to be aware of current social conventions when confronting subjects about their behavior. For some, being told their behavior is unacceptable by a "security guard" may be the lowest form of social insult. Security personnel need to take these social realities and public perceptions seriously and integrate them into their conflict resolution strategies.

When security personnel are attempting to resolve conflict involving uncooperative subjects, they need to appeal to a subject's ethical and moral or pragmatic motivations. The use of social-psychological compliance-gaining motivations or other motivational techniques used at each step of the negotiating subject cooperation process may improve the likelihood of creating a productive environment in which voluntary cooperation can flourish.

Timeliness also plays an important role in the successful application of verbal conflict resolution strategies. To move efficiently through the negotiating subject cooperation process, personnel need to avoid being snared in power struggles with uncooperative subjects. Personnel need to complete the negotiating subject cooperation steps in an efficient and timely manner.[12] If the process moves too slowly or if the security personnel/subject interaction begins at a heighted emotional state, a power struggle may ensue. Power struggles often lead to entrenched physical behaviors and have the potential to quickly escalate to violence. If an uncooperative subject becomes entrenched in his refusal to cooperate with security personnel,

---

[11] Developing and practicing a series of acceptable/authorized verbal scripts may be helpful.

[12] Efficiency should not be confused with rushing through the process in order to use physical conflict resolution strategies.

the interaction may need to be reassigned to another responsible internal or external stakeholder for resolution.[13]

Interpersonal Field Conflict Dynamics

Nonphysical, communicative-based conflict resolution strategies are generally effective only when applied to passive-aggressive subjects at the initial stage of interpersonal field conflict but not at higher levels of interpersonal field conflict. Attempts to resolve conflict without considering the unique *interpersonal field conflict dynamics* that exist between the involved parties may lead to the premature use of higher levels of force and physical injuries.

The interpersonal field conflict dynamics are the social-psychological conditions that exist between the conflicted parties at the time that conflict resolution strategies are introduced into the interaction. The subject contact stage and the behavioral phase are the two most important interpersonal field conflict dynamics.

There are two subject contact stages, initial and secondary, and three behavioral phases, passive-aggressive, direct aggression, or active violence. Verbal tactics are primarily effective when applied at the initial contact stage of passive-aggressive behavior. However, in interacting with directly aggressive behavior at the multiple contact stage or in dealing with actively violent subjects, communicative solutions are ineffective and personnel will have no choice but to use physical conflict resolution strategies.[14]

The DEACONS Approach

We've developed a proprietary verbal tactics conflict resolution system that's effective at the initial contact stage/passive-aggressive behavioral phase. It is called DEACONS: The Seven Steps to Negotiating Subject Cooperation. The use of a systematic approach to negotiating subject cooperation, like the DEACONS system, greatly increases the likelihood that subjects will submit to security personnel's request for cooperation. We use the acronym DEACONS to help security personnel remember the seven-step process to *negotiating subject cooperation* (NSC):

1. **D**ialogue with the subject.
2. **E**xplain the conflict.
3. **A**sk for cooperation.
4. **C**ontext: Identify the law, policy, or basis for the conflict.

---

[13] See Chapter 3 for a more detailed exposition of accessing and assigning stakeholders.
[14] See Chapter 3 for a more information on interpersonal conflict dynamics.

5. **O**ptions and outcomes: Present the spectrum of conflict resolution options and corresponding outcomes.
6. **N**egotiate with the subject.
7. **S**ettle: One- or two-party agreement.

STEP ONE: DIALOGUE WITH A SUBJECT

Dialogue is the most important step in the NSC process. Security personnel must be able to initiate and maintain productive conversations in order to develop a relational base that's necessary for influencing subject behavior. The ability to develop a relational base is the key to negotiating successful outcomes. Dialogue assists security personnel by helping them socially connect with initially resistant subjects and develop credibility.

Dialogue is the casual or informal (but professional) banter that's developed between security personnel and subjects for the purpose of creating a temporary relational base in order to influence their behavior.

Security personnel establish credibility through verbal tactics and command presence. Security personnel who are able to create this relational base are more successful at de-escalating highly charged emotions and resolving conflict without the need to use physical force.[15]

Step Two: Explain the Nature of the Conflict

If security personnel are successful at creating an effective relational base and the subject is predisposed to cooperation, the subject will respond positively to security personnel *after* they explain the nature of the conflict. However, if those conditions are not met the subject will likely resist. If the subject fails to cooperate, move to step three.

Step Three: Ask for Cooperation

Step three is the first opportunity in the NSC process for security personnel to ask for cooperation. Only *after* developing credibility through verbal tactics and command presence and after explaining the nature of the conflict should security personnel ask the subject to start or stop some desired action. If security personnel are effective at creating a relational base and the subject is predisposed to cooperation, the subject will respond positively to the security personnel's request for cooperation. However, if those conditions are not met, the subject will likely remain uncooperative. Security personnel need to ask for cooperation after each *succeeding*

---

[15] Since some security personnel find it difficult to initiate conversations with subjects, it may be useful to develop a set of *written verbal scripts* to assist security personnel in *jump-starting* conversations.

step in the NSC process. If the subject fails to cooperate at any step, move to the next step.[16]

Step Four: Context

Identify the policy, procedure, rule, or law that applies to the specific subject interaction.

Even typically uncooperative subjects will often cooperate after security personnel explain in *detail* how their behavior contradicts a policy, procedure, rule, law, or other specific conditions. Passive-aggressive individuals fall into this category and require a great deal of patience and understanding to maintain control of the conflict. If the subject fails to cooperate, move to step five.

Step Five: Options and Outcomes

Explain and describe the possible conflict resolution options and outcomes.

When explaining and describing the available conflict resolution options and outcomes, security personnel should present the positive and the negative outcomes of each option. Personnel should always start by presenting the positive outcomes for cooperating before moving on to the negative consequences. Prior to presenting the potential negative outcomes for being uncooperative, security personnel should carefully consider the limits of their authority. Personnel should always look to be as creative as possible when providing available options to uncooperative subjects. If the subject fails to cooperate, move to step six.

Step Six: Negotiate a Settlement

Negotiation is the give-and-take process that takes place between two or more parties, each with their own aims, needs, and viewpoints, seeking to discover common ground and reach an agreement to settle a matter of mutual concern or a conflict. Negotiating could be as simple as telling a driver her vehicle is parked in an unauthorized location but you'll allow it to remain there for an additional five minutes before taking action; or it could be as unsophisticated as using the NSC process to deflect verbal abuse by leaving the immediate area.

Negotiated agreements *should not* create additional safety concerns for the uncooperative subject, other community members, or security individuals.

Step Seven: Settle with the Subject

After negotiating with the subject, complete the process by deciding on and finalizing a course of action. Settling may or may not include the other party's agreement. Settlement may mean that the security individual submits to the will of the

---

[16]Most security personnel/subject interactions will end at step three. However, if the first three NSC steps are ineffective, personnel should move on to the following steps in the process.

uncooperative subject, or it may mean that the security personnel assert their limited authority and take decisive protective action *without* consulting the subject. Security personnel should try to verbally confirm the subject's choice, repeat the corresponding outcome, and give the subject a final opportunity to cooperate before initiating physical intervention.

Prior to application of protective action, security personnel need to be sure they're acting within their departmental policy, have requisite legal authority, and have the physical ability to force an uncooperative subject to comply with their commands.

Verbal Aggression

The use of verbal tactics to negotiate subject cooperation requires a comprehensive understanding of an organization's safety mission, patience, self-discipline, and self-control. This is especially true when security personnel are being verbally attacked while trying to process complicated and constantly evolving circumstances. Generally speaking, security personnel cannot apply protective action against a verbally abusive subject. To justify the application of protective action, a subject must be an immediate or active physical threat, to others or themselves, or physically resistant when security personnel lawfully attempt to control or restrain them. To effectively manage verbal abuse, security personnel must *depersonalize* the subject's verbal assaults. If security personnel fail to depersonalize verbal abuse, it may create emotions that lead to a loss of self-control and the application of inappropriate or unlawful protective action.

Communication Strategies for Dealing with Verbal Aggression

- *Deflect it.* Security personnel need to understand that a subject's verbal abuse is not directed at them but rather at their perceived authority.
- *Acknowledge hearing it.* Security personnel could acknowledge the subject's concerns without agreeing with his or her statements.
- *Redirect it.* Security personnel should use verbal tactics and command presence to refocus the subject's attention back to the cooperative task at hand.

When security personnel are faced with verbal aggressiveness, their goal should be negotiating subject cooperation, *not* the enforcement of laws, policies, or rules.

Perception Management

The effective use of verbal tactics also involves managing the public's perceptions. There's truth in the adage, "Perception is reality." Security personnel should always strive to act in an ethical manner, and they need to consider how their specific actions may be perceived by organizational or community members. Sometimes it is best *not* to take an action, even if an action is ethical. When security personnel use verbal tactics, they need to be perceived as serious but as flexible as possible in communicating their conflict resolution goals. When dealing with field conflict, the public expects security personnel to display a much higher level of patience, self-control, and understanding than they do with the general public.

While trying to negotiate subject cooperation, security personnel should never get into a "push-and-pull" debate with uncooperative subjects. Power struggles can create unsafe conditions for security personnel and others in proximity to the conflict. Security personnel should never communicate ultimatums ("or else" statements) to subjects they're not able to legally, ethically, or practically follow through on.

Summary

A successful organizational safety program depends on competent communicators. Verbal strategies for resolving conflict are the most important protective theories, techniques, and tactics. Since most conflict can be managed and resolved verbally, without the need to use physical force, all security personnel should become competent in verbal conflict resolution strategies. However, when words fail, personnel need to know that they are able to use protective action to resolve interpersonal conflict.

RECOMMENDATIONS

1. Train security personnel in the core competencies of verbal conflict resolution.

References

Edley, C.F., and Robinson, C. F. "Response to Protests on UC Campuses." Report draft for public comment, 4 May 2012.Web: http://campusprotestreport.universityofcalifornia.edu, 5 May 2012.

Henning, Kathy "Assessing Levels of Power: Wisconsin Technical College System." 8 May 2012. Web: www.wisc-online.com, 8 May 2011.

Tracey, Wallach, 2004. "Transforming Conflict: A Group Relations Perspective." Peace and Conflict Studies vol. 11–1, 81–92.

Chapter 11

Physical Conflict Resolution Strategies: Theories, Techniques, Tactics, and Tools for Resolving Conflict

The Problem

Security personnel aren't adequately trained in the use of physical conflict resolution strategies.

Introduction

An effective organizational safety program must include the option for security personnel to use physical conflict resolution strategies, including protective theories, techniques, tactics, and tools to resolve conflict. Although most interpersonal field conflict can be resolved through effective verbal communication, there are times when it's necessary for personnel to use physical protective strategies to resolve conflict and maintain safe organizations.

121

Process

For security personnel to effectively resolve field conflict, they need to be trained in the full spectrum of verbal and physical conflict resolution strategies. Unfortunately, since many organizations have enacted noncontact or restrictive use-of-force policies, some falsely assume that security personnel don't need to be trained in physical conflict resolution strategies. This basic misunderstanding of the nature of conflict has the potential to create unsafe working conditions and decrease organizational and community safety.[1]

It's true that unlike verbal strategies, the use of physical conflict strategies may lead to physical injuries; this possibility scares many senior stakeholders. However, it's impossible to create safe organizations *without* occasionally resorting to the use of protective action.

Authority and Jurisdiction

To safely and legally utilize protective theories, techniques, tactics, or tools to resolve conflict, security personnel need to understand the limits of their authority and power.

In the private market, an organization's jurisdiction or area of responsibility is limited to the property it owns or to the property it controls. Private security personnel function as *agents* of the owner; therefore, they have the same behavioral limits as the owner or the party responsible for the property to which the personnel are assigned. In short, if it's legal for the owner to act, it's legal for private security personnel to act. The owner's activities are limited by the laws that govern the owner's specific jurisdiction.

An organization's policies and procedures are the primary source of a security individual's limited authority, power, and permission to act (or a prohibition from acting) during interpersonal field conflict. Since criminal statutes provide a limited framework for guiding private (non-sworn) security personnel behavior, organizations typically create their own limits in an attempt to mitigate civil liability. These limitations may or may not actually mitigate claims of negligence because claims are the result of both acting and failing to act. Forbidding action only mitigates potential liability resulting from unreasonable actions. However, they do nothing to mitigate negligence claims created from falling to act.[2] Although "private person" authority is addressed in various legal codes[3] and social compacts and through situational ethics, the bottom line is that it's up to the employing organization to determine the appropriate security personnel behavioral boundaries.

---

[1] See Chapter 6 for a more detailed exposition of the nature of conflict.
[2] See Chapter 7 for a more detailed exposition of liability and negligence.
[3] See California Penal Codes 834, 835, 837, 839, 841, 844, 845, or 846 for details on private person limits.

Law Enforcement Versus Private Security Personnel Authority

Since private security personnel are not government actors, much of the typical use-of-force literature that's been misapplied in private-market contexts will be omitted here. However, gaining a basic understanding of the use-of-force distinctions between law enforcement and private security personnel is important. Since security personnel are not government employees, they cannot ordinarily violate a subject's civil or constitutional rights. However, this doesn't mean that certain behavior, in extreme cases, couldn't violate a law or cause a civil action to be initiated against the security individual or vicariously through that individual's employer.

In 1989 (*Graham v. Connor*) the U.S. Supreme Court developed a constitutional standard to evaluate law enforcement use-of-force challenges.[4] The court established an objective standard to measure the reasonableness of using physical force. Although the objectiveness test specifically applies to government-employed law enforcement officers, it's a useful and rational guide to help the private security industry better understand the role that force[5] plays in protecting people.

GRAHAM V. CONNOR: THE STANDARD

1. Judged from the perspective of the officer.
2. Examined through the eyes of an officer on the scene at the time force is applied.
3. Based on the facts and circumstances confronting the officer without regard to the personnel's underlying intent or motivation.
4. Based on the knowledge that the officer acted properly under the established law at the time.

NONCONSENSUAL PHYSICAL CONTACT

Unlike law enforcement personnel, non-sworn private security personnel have narrower limits for making physical contact with unarrested subjects without their expressed consent. Physical contact with an unarrested subject should only be initiated for protective purposes. In some circumstances the subject's affiliation status[6] may provide greater latitude for nonconsensual contact.[7] Generally, to justify

---

[4] U.S. Supreme Court, *Graham v. Connor*, 490. US 286 (1989), No. 87-6571.

[5] We prefer the term *protective action* rather than the word *force* to describe private security personnel's physical interactions with resistant subjects.

[6] See Chapter 3 for a full exposition of interpersonal conflict dynamics.

[7] For example, personnel are allowed to make physical contact with students who had previously signed a student's *standard of conduct agreement* that contained certain stipulations, including allowing for physical searches.

making physical subject contact, including personal contact necessary for the application of protective techniques, tactics or tools, subjects are required to be:

1. An immediate physical threat to the security personnel, others, or themselves.
2. An active physical threat to security personnel, others, or themselves.
3. Placed under arrest for a serious nonproperty[8] related criminal violation (e.g., battery or sexual assault) when it's in the best of interest of the organization to control and restrain the subject and turn them over to a law enforcement agency for prosecution.

Absent legal, ethical, and moral justification for making physical contact with an unarrested subject, security personnel who make nonconsensual contact may create unnecessary civil liability.

Protective Action

To determine the quality and quantity of protective action that's necessary and reasonable to achieve their conflict resolution goals, security personnel must evaluate the totality of the circumstances known to them at the time of the subject interaction.

The decision to use protective action must be made through objective and reasonable means, and the strategies personnel employ must be evaluated by their potential effectiveness.

We define *protective action* as physical subject contact, whether it's accomplished through personal body contact or with a protective device or tool, for the narrow purpose of protecting individuals (including security personnel, employees, or others) from immediate or active physical harm, applied in a manner that minimizes potential injury and maximizes safety for all involved subjects.

To justify the application of protective action, personnel must objectively analyze the subject's resistance (SR) level before applying the appropriate and reasonable level of protective action. Effectiveness is judged by comparing potential conflict resolution outcomes against an organization's safety mission. The security individual's chosen protective action must have a high probability of creating an *effective* conflict resolution outcome.

A Matter of Degree: Force Versus Resistance

The *subject's resistance* (SR) is the primary factor for deciding the appropriate protective action option. Initially, security personnel are at tactical disadvantage

---

[8] Due to their inherent physical danger, we don't recommend trying to make property crime-related arrests.

because they're forced to react *defensively* to a subject's offensive physical actions. This conflict reality is a stark reminder that security personnel need to be prepared (and authorized) to use a multitude of protective actions for resolving aggressive or assaultive behavior.

The application of protective action must be reasonable compared to the subject's resistance and reasonable to the context of the conflict. The reasonableness standard is evaluated by comparing the personnel's protective actions against the way other similarly situated security personnel would have responded given the same or similar circumstances. The reasonableness standard is not a hindsight standard.[9]

▮ Justifying Physical Contact

Although there's no exhaustive and authoritative list to justify the application of protective action, the following are useful guidelines to assist security personnel in determining the best protective action option in any given situation: objective criteria, subject/security personnel interaction factors, security personnel/subject interaction factors, subject behavioral factors, environmental conditions, and situational factors.

OBJECTIVE CRITERIA (NONEXHAUSTIVE LIST)

1. Amount and nature of the resistance observed or perceived
2. The type and severity of the crime
3. Subject is armed or has access to weapons
4. Subject not submitting peacefully
5. Knowledge/history of the subject
6. Immediacy and probability of threats to life

SUBJECT/SECURITY PERSONNEL INTERACTION FACTORS

1. Subject's potential state of mind
2. Health or mental crisis
3. Diminished mental or psychological capacity
4. Under the influence of drugs or alcohol
5. Immature, infirm, or elderly
6. Physical size
7. Specialized training (e.g., trained fighter)
8. Housing challenged

---

[9] Also see *Graham v. Connor.*

SECURITY PERSONNEL/SUBJECT INTERACTION FACTORS

1. Security personnel's state of mind
2. Training
3. Experience
4. Knowledge
5. Physical condition/injury or exhaustion
6. Emotional stability

SUBJECT BEHAVIORAL FACTORS (NONEXHAUSTIVE LIST)

1. Stated verbal disagreement
2. Threats of physical attack
3. Profanities
4. Challenges to fight
5. Expressed refusal to follow verbal commands
6. Obscene gestures
7. Assuming an aggressive or fighting stance
8. Damaging physical property

ENVIRONMENTAL CONDITIONS (NONEXHAUSTIVE LIST)

1. *Standing or footing.* What's the terrain like—stairs, steps, porch, balcony, furniture, slick floors, curbs, gutters, parking bumpers, landscaping, sloping, uneven ground, gravel, sand, vehicle traffic, or ground affected by weather conditions such as rain, ice, or snow?
2. *Number of subjects.* Anyone in the immediate area, including bystanders, may also be friends of the subject
3. *Availability of assistance.* Backup from other security personnel or from law enforcement officers.
4. *Access to cover.* The ability to reach the closest objects that can be used for suitable cover.

OTHER PERSONNEL CONSIDERATIONS

1. Knowledge, understanding, experience, and training in high-conflict situations/
2. Physical condition, strength, fitness level, self-defense or use-of-force expertise, and confidence in the application of force.

SITUATIONAL FACTORS (NONEXHAUSTIVE LIST)

1. *Severity of crime.* Nonviolent misdemeanor, violent misdemeanor, nonviolent felony, or violent felony.
2. *Timing of crime.* In progress, immediate post-assault, or stale.
3. *Multiple subjects.* More than one subject, active or passive subjects.
4. *Subject's relative physical strength.* An obviously physically fit subject.
5. *Subject/security personnel proximity.* The physical distance between the parties; the closer the gap, the greater the possibility for potential injury.
6. *Time/decision ratio.* How urgent is the need to act? Compare the difference between a subject that's actively charging at security individual versus a subject held up for hours in a hostage situation.
7. *History/prior subject knowledge.* The security personnel has previous knowledge or previous contact with the subject.
8. *Proximity to physical weapons.* Actual weapon, e.g., knives or firearms; improvised weapon, e.g., pipes, bats, broken glass, rocks.
9. *Security personnel on the ground.* Security personnel and/or subjects are not standing up. This creates a much greater physical danger for personnel.
10. *Physical environment.* Hot, cold, wet, flat, uneven, hilly, obstacles, grass, gravel, cement, sunny, or dark.
11. *Social-political environment.* Cultural, racial, ethnic, gender, or other considerations.
12. *Mobs/riots/protestors.* Large out-of-control groups with a unifying goal or message.

Situational Protective Action Risk Continuum (SPARC)

Force Decisions Institute has developed a proprietary private-person, protective use-of-force continuum exclusively for managing and resolving private-market interpersonal field conflict. The Situational Protective Action Risk Continuum (SPARC)[10] is a graphic visual representation of the protective-action decision-making process (Figure 11.1). The chart is a visual aid used to depict the legal, ethical, and departmental considerations for a security individual's protective actions. It is also intended to enhance security personnel knowledge and understanding of the proper use and application of protective action under rapidly changing circumstances.

---

[10] Formerly known as a use-of-force continuum.

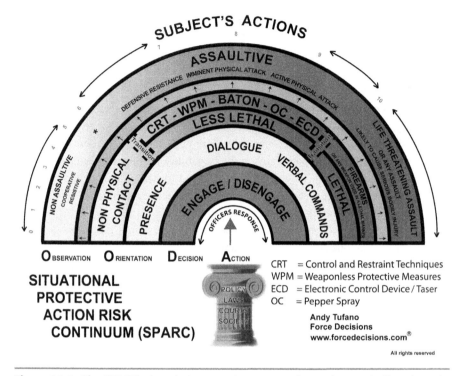

SITUATIONAL
PROTECTIVE
ACTION RISK
CONTINUUM (SPARC)

CRT = Control and Restraint Techniques
WPM = Weaponless Protective Measures
ECD = Electronic Control Device / Taser
OC = Pepper Spray

Andy Tufano
Force Decisions
www.forcedecisions.com®

Figure 11.1. The SPARC chart helps security personnel correlate and align the subject's resistance to the appropriate protective-action option.

Aligning Situational Force

SUBJECT'S ACTIONS: DEFINED

Since security personnel response is a reaction to a subject's behavior, personnel have to quickly access and determine, to the best of their ability, the subject's resistance level.

Subject resistance (SR) is divided into three levels: nonassaultive, assaultive, and lethal. The subject's *relative* resistance is rated numerically on scale of 0–10, the higher number representing the greater level of resistance or risk.

There are also three correlated Protective Action Response Zones (PARZs): nonphysical contact, less lethal contact, and lethal contact.

Subject Resistance (SR) Levels

LEVEL I: NONASSAULTIVE

Cooperative or resistive; SR ranging from 0–5.9.

Cooperative

Some people may fall into this category. At this level the subject complies with verbal commands and directions. Subjects respond positively to security personnel command presence and verbal tactics. They offer no resistance, and no physical contact or protective action is necessary.

Resistive

Subjects may present verbal and passive physical resistance that indicates they *won't* cooperate. This type of resistance may include mild or aggressive verbal communication such as stated verbal disagreement, threats of physical attack, profanities, or challenges to fight. Passive physical resistance may include refusal to follow verbal commands, obscene gestures, or assuming an aggressive or fighting stance. At this level the subject is *not* an immediate physical threat or an active physical threat to security personnel or third parties, and no physical contact or protective action is authorized.

Possible protective action includes tactical retreat, command presence, dialogue and verbal commands, and transferring responsibility to other responsible stakeholders (such as administrators or law enforcement personnel).

LEVEL II: ASSAULTIVE

SR ranging from 6.0–9.9.

At this level the subject presents an immediate physical attack, commits an active physical attack, or presents defensive resistance during an attempt to control or restrain a subject, which may quickly escalate to a physical assault.

In these scenarios the subject has crossed the *noncontact* resistance threshold and protective action is authorized. It's likely that personnel or a third party may be injured. Security personnel will need to apply protective action to minimize potential injury to security personnel or other involved parties.

Possible protective action includes tactical retreat, CRT, WPM, baton, OC, or Taser.

LEVEL III: LIFE-THREATENING ASSAULT

SR range 10.

At this level the subject commits a physical attack capable of causing serious bodily injury or death.

This category includes subject actions that are likely to result in serious injury or possible death to personnel or third parties.

Possible protective action includes tactical retreat, firearm, or use of any protective technique, tactic, or tool in a lethal manner.

Dealing with Immediate Physical Threats

A subject is considered an immediate physical threat when he or she verbally communicates and/or physically communicates an intention to physically attack security personnel, a third party, or him- or herself and the personnel interpreting these behaviors reasonably determine—through a quick, fact-based assessment of known objective behavioral and situational factors—that failing to intervene or act will lead to security personnel, third parties, or the subject being injured.

Security personnel need to articulate *objective* factors, not *possible* factors, which cause them to believe that a subject is an immediate threat. Objective factors to justify the application of protective action include both behavioral and situational factors. Different personnel faced with the same situation may choose different, but appropriate, protective-action options.

Security personnel must avoid using purely subjective factors to access the potentiality of a physical assault. "I thought the subject may have had a weapon" is not sufficient justification for the application of protective action. Only objective factors (behavioral and situational) justify the application of protective action.

The subject's resistance will determine the protective action options that personnel should apply to subject interaction. The available protective action options are contained within each PARZ. Protective action options are applied based on the amount or degree of resistance the subject presents as well as other relevant conditions or circumstances surrounding the specific subject interaction.

Before personnel apply protective action to subject resistance, they must complete the *observation, orientation, decision, and action* (OODA) cycle. The final stage of the OODA cycle, the action stage, is the entry point into the SPARC.

Prior to taking protective action, personnel must process the various environmental stimuli through the OODA loop. The bottom of the SPARC chart depicts personnel entering the protective action continuum after processing the OODA loop.

The OODA loop, often called *Boyd's cycle*, is a creation of Col. John Boyd, USAF (Ret.). Col. Boyd was a student of tactical operations who observed similarities in many military battles and campaigns (Hammonds). He observed that in many engagements, one side presented the other with a series of unexpected and threatening stimuli, and the opposite side wasn't able to keep pace with them. The quicker side eventually succeeded. Col. Boyd observed a basic conflict axiom: Conflicts are *time competitive*.

Since all tactical environments are dynamic, they're naturally time sensitive. Decisions and actions that are delayed are often ineffective because of the constantly changing circumstances. When an adversary is involved, as in a field conflict, the operation is not only time sensitive but also time competitive. Time or opportunity neglected by one adversary can be potentially exploited by the other.

The adversary that can complete this cycle faster than the other gains a tremendous tactical advantage. By the time the slower adversary reacts, the faster one is doing something different and the reaction becomes ineffective. With each cycle, the slower party's action is exponentially more ineffective by a growing and widening margin.

Protective Action Response Zones (PARZ)

We've divided security personnel responses into three zones correlated to the subject's resistance (SR) levels, 0–10. Within each of these three protective-action zones, personnel have various force options. Some protective-action zone options may not be available, or they may be more or less effective or more or less acceptable, depending on the protective tool array that security personnel carry, including their tactical knowledge, the actual circumstances, or the departmental policy.

For instance, in Zone Two, there are five protective action options. Security personnel need to justify their reasoning for using a specific protective action option in *that* particular PARZ as opposed to others. Some use-of-force policies may dictate that security personnel prioritize protective-action options within each of these zones. Personnel should always consider behavioral and situational factors and departmental policy before choosing a protective-action option.

PARZ One: Noncontact

PARZ One is a noncontact area. In this zone, security personnel are not authorized to make physical contact with a subject. Protective action should only be utilized after attempts to negotiate subject cooperation fail or if they're an inappropriate option for the given context.

PARZ Two: Less Lethal

Weaponless Options

The following are protective weaponless techniques and tactics that should be available to all security personnel.

CRT: Control and Restraint Techniques

These are protective tactics and techniques used to control and restrain assaultive individuals or individuals who have committed serious criminal acts and will be turned over to law enforcement for prosecution. These techniques include physical control holds and the application of physical restraints (e.g., handcuffs).

We've modified the typical arrest-and-control (ACT) techniques to accommodate our protective philosophies. We call this modified course "Control and Restraint

Tactics (CRT)." Our course prohibits closed-fist strikes to the face while discouraging police-type control techniques typically known as *distraction strikes*. This approach protects private security personnel, community members, and organization reputations and doesn't interfere with an organization's primary business operations.

WPM: Weaponless Protective Measures

These are weaponless tactics and techniques used to protect individuals against unarmed physical assaults. These weaponless protective measures are used to protect personnel against punches, grabs, or kicks, with a focus on transitioning to the protective tools or devices that security personnel carry.[11]

Protective Tools or Devices

The following are protective tools and devices that are available to security personnel.

OC/Pepper Spray

The use of protective aerosol irritants is an effective self-protection option that fits appropriately into a protective organizational safety philosophy.

Baton

The baton could be an effective protective device, but it also has the potential to create unnecessary liability. Baton use should be limited to defensive or protective use only. Its primary use should be for blocking physical assaults; only under narrow and exigent circumstances should it be used as an impact device.

Long ago, security departments adopted this police weapon into their defensive tool/device array. However, since the baton has the potential to create unnecessary civil and criminal liability we recommend placing limits on its use. In California, the baton is considered a dangerous weapon under CA PC 12020 (a), and it's a felony to possess one without appropriate training, licensing, and a legitimate legal purpose.

ECD or Taser®

Electronic control devices (ECDs) are used to control and restrain assaultive individuals. ECDs are currently the most effective protective device available to private security personnel. One of the many advantages of an ECD is that it can be used in three protective modes: verbal reference, display, or actual use. It's the only tool or

---

[11] Force Decisions Institute has developed a unique and proprietary protective tactics system that integrates protective organizational safety principles into a weaponless self-defense system that mitigates negligence claims typically associated with physical intervention.

device that protects organizations, personnel, and resistant subjects without creating any long-lasting physical injuries. Because an ECD is the most effective tool that non-sworn security personnel can legally carry and because it fits perfectly into a protective organizational safety philosophy, we support and encourage organizations to allow their security personnel to carry and use ECDs.[12]

PARZ Three: Lethal

These are the tactics and techniques used to protect against life-threatening physical assaults through the lethal use of protective tactics and tools. Security personnel may use any protective tool or any object or tactic to resist life-threatening attacks. Since the majority of private-person security personnel don't carry firearms, it's important for personnel to understand the limitations of their less lethal protective tools and to understand how these tactics or tools may be used in a lethal manner.

Firearm
These are tactics and techniques used to protect against life-threatening physical assaults through the lethal use of a handgun.

Summary

Physical conflict resolution strategies play an important role in resolving field conflict and maintaining safe organizations. Physical conflict resolution strategies improve personnel and organizational and community safety and mitigate potential liability.

RECOMMENDATIONS

1. Train security personnel in a full spectrum of verbal and physical conflict resolution strategies, including protective theories, techniques, tactics, and tools.

---

[12]The only ECD we recommend is made by Taser International.

Chapter 12

Security Personnel Accountability

The Problem

Organizations don't have a reliable accountability method for evaluating their security personnel's use of protective action.

Introduction

Accountability plays an important role in successful conflict resolution. Organizations with responsible and effective policies and procedures need to hold security personnel accountable for the decision to use or refrain from using physical conflict resolution strategies. Since the decision to use physical conflict resolution strategies could create potential liability for an organization, organizations need to require legal and ethical justifications for their use.

Although most people think of accountability in the negative, justifying an action that *was* made, a decision to *not* act also needs accounting. The choice to use physical conflict resolution strategies needs to be accountable to the organization, the security department, other vested stakeholders, and community members. Holding security personnel accountable for their conflict resolution decisions plays an important role in maintaining safe organizations.

Today more than ever, communities are sensitive to and focused on ensuring that individuals who interact with an organization's security personnel are treated fairly, even when the resistant subject's behavior is criminal. The only way to ensure that people are treated fairly while guaranteeing the effectiveness of an organization's approved conflict resolution strategies is to hold personnel accountable.

Process

In today's society, the decision to use protective action in a private setting to resolve conflict is a sensitive matter. However, an organization's or community's sensitivities should not be justification for avoiding the use of physical protective action if it's necessary and appropriate for a given situation. Whenever security personnel use physical action or fail to use physical action when it's necessary, they need to be held accountable.

Documentation

Professionalism dictates that security personnel justify their protective-action decisions both verbally and in writing. When protective action has been employed, the security individual's written report must include the critical interaction information needed to ensure the chronology and the details of the events, including a full accounting of the involved parties' actions. Failure to accurately detail a resistant subject's physical actions and the security individual's decision to use physical action may result in an inaccurate interpretation of the field conflict. This is important since physical interactions between security personnel and uncooperative subjects are some of the most scrutinized interpersonal activities in the security industry.

When personnel follow their organization's protective-action policy and they're characterized by responsible decision making, those personnel shouldn't be concerned about being scrutinized for their decision to take action. Any experienced security individual can provide numerous examples in which security personnel were unfairly disciplined or fired for using physical force to resolve interpersonal field conflict. Whether these stories are accurate, anecdotal, or purely perceptual, there is universal skepticism about any system of accountability.

Unfortunately, most security personnel have difficulty documenting their decision-making processes and their actions in a professionally written report.[1] It's extremely important for personnel to accurately describe (in fine detail) the subject's specific acts in their full context and their own responsive use of protective action.

Even when security personnel are justified in their actions, they often create unwarranted criticism for their protective-action choices because they're unable to clearly justify their actions in an acceptable written format.

Security Staff Accountability

If security personnel exceed their limited authority and use inappropriate protective action, they can be criminally prosecuted, be civilly sued, lose their employment, or create dissention in their community. Moreover, security personnel are not exempt from being criminally prosecuted if they violate criminal codes.

Inappropriate use of protective action can lead to security personnel being civilly sued for behavior that falls short of criminal culpability but is still inappropriate. Through vicarious civil liability, the security personnel's employer or other corporate personnel can also be drawn into a civil action created by the security individual's inappropriate actions. The consequences of a civil action are personal financial judgments and a possible financial judgment against a security employee's employer. The application of inappropriate protective action can lead to security personnel being disciplined, up to and including loss of employment.

Interpersonal cooperation plays an important role in the creation and maintenance of safe and secure organizations. To be effective, security personnel need to gain the cooperation of the communities they serve. The inappropriate use of protective action can create community dissention. If community members feel mistreated, security personnel lose their moral and ethical standing and subsequently the community's trust. It's impossible to maintain high levels of safety when large segments of the organization and community perceive security personnel as their adversaries. When security personnel are confronted by uncooperative subjects, the best way to avoid alienating organizational and community members is to follow the organization's policies and procedures.

Peer Intervention

To hold security personnel accountable for their protective-action decisions, personnel may need to intervene if others lose their emotional self-control. Since

---

[1] As a college professor I can attest that this is not unique to security personnel! Many college students also struggle to perform basic writing tasks.

community members expect to be treated fairly, they also expect other security personnel and other nonsecurity stakeholders to intervene if inappropriate protective action is applied.

Peer intervention is an activity that prevents or stops inappropriate or unlawful physical contact or assaultive behavior. Peer intervention affords personnel an opportunity to maintain or restore their professionalism. Although there's no exhaustive list of behaviors that may require personnel to intervene, some of those behaviors include:

■ Inappropriate or unlawful application of force
■ Other unethical, inappropriate behavior

The failure of personnel to intervene may lead to decreases in personnel safety, professionalism, and credibility. Peer intervention protects personnel from:

■ Civil liability
■ Criminal action
■ Creating negative attitudes about the security industry
■ Customer service complaints
■ Disciplinary action
■ Loss of personal integrity
■ Loss of professionalism
■ Physical injury

Appropriate peer intervention involves various (and sensitive) techniques for protecting community members and restoring or maintaining professional behavior during interpersonal field conflict. Depending on the specific circumstances of each contact, it may be necessary to intervene immediately; in other instances, it may be wise to wait until after the interaction. When being verbally assaulted or witnessing someone being physically attacked, it is normal for personnel to experience strong emotions toward uncooperative subjects. These emotions may be even stronger when a partner security individual is being physically assaulted.

These strong emotions may influence some security personnel to enter the OODA cycle[2] in an emotionally unstable manner, increasing the possibility of applying inappropriate protective action without the security individual even realizing it. Security personnel need to immediately intervene under these conditions in order to protect all interested parties. In some instances, departmental policy may dictate that peer interventions be reported to supervisors.

Under certain circumstances, it may be appropriate to apply immediate peer intervention techniques such as verbal, physical touch, or even physical restraint. If security personnel become agitated or angry or appear to be losing professional

---

[2] See Chapter 11 for a fuller exposition of the OODA loop.

objectivity during a field interaction, a peer can assist by telling the offending security individual that they'll take charge of the interaction.

If security personnel are engaged in a heated verbal confrontation with a subject and start to become increasingly agitated, a peer could lightly touch the security individual and offer a tactful reminder to calm down or offer to take over responsibility for the interaction.

If security personnel use unlawful or clearly unreasonable force, a peer may be required to physically take hold of the offending security individual and physically separate that person from the subject.

In situations that have already taken place, it may be necessary to implement a delayed peer intervention technique. This type of response can be a valuable technique for improving professionalism. Some delayed peer intervention techniques include discussion, admonishment, or offering training advice. If a security individual is verbally condescending to a subject, a peer can casually discuss the inappropriateness of the behavior. If security personnel use inappropriate or demeaning language while interacting with organizational or community members, a peer could inform the offending security individual that his or her behavior is unacceptable and may end up exacerbating the situation.

Factors Affecting Personnel Intervention

Although security personnel are ethically, morally, and possibly, through departmental policy, obligated to intervene when they observe inappropriate behavior by a peer, personal and emotional circumstances may prevent security personnel from intervening. Personnel may fail to take action when a peer is behaving inappropriately because of several factors, including:

- Anger
- Conflict avoidance
- Diffusion of responsibility ("It's not my fault!")
- Evaluation apprehension
- Fear of being ostracized
- Fear of physical harm
- Incompetence
- Misplaced loyalty
- Peer pressure
- Situational ignorance

If security personnel witness a peer resorting to or on the verge of behaving inappropriately, the observing personnel should take appropriate action by intervening. This requires making a rational decision about the offending individual's inability to make the right choice in the heat of the moment. Such behavior may include inappropriate use of language or profanity, other unlawful or inappropriate behavior, or the unlawful or inappropriate application of protective action.

Intervention also demonstrates personal integrity, enhances personnel and organizational safety, preserves professionalism, strengthens community confidence in the organization's safety mission, and reduces personal and corporate civil liability.[3]

Responsible personnel supervision is an important component of an effective and accountable conflict resolution strategy. Supervisors need to monitor their subordinates' performance to ensure they're adhering to the organization's conflict resolution policies and procedures, maintaining the department's minimum personnel productivity standard, treating the community with respect, and not creating unnecessary liability. Ideally, supervisors should be conflict resolution experts and be exemplary role models for their subordinates to emulate.

Post-Incident Review and Reporting Process

An effective and responsible use-of-force policy must include a fair and thorough post-incident review process. The organization, community members, and security personnel depend on a fair and accountable use of a protective-action post-incident review process. The post-incident review process achieves the following:

- Affords organizations an opportunity to determine whether their policies and procedures are effective at creating safe organizations while minimizing potential financial exposure.
- Allows organizational and community members to feel confident that security personnel are treating individuals with dignity.
- Assures security personnel that their protective-action use will be fairly evaluated.

Using Metrics as an Element of Accountability

One of the most challenging components of creating a fair and reliable protective-action review process is determining an appropriate standard against which to measure its use. Two standards are generally used to evaluate protective-action decision making: hindsight and situational metrics. Unfortunately, the inevitability, unavoidability, and unpredictability of conflict create social, political, and financial pressures that often interfere with a fair protective-action evaluation process. These pressures

---

[3] This section is based on the principles drawn from California POST Learning Domain 20, Chapter 6, "Intervention."

often create a disincentive for senior stakeholders to defend their security personnel's protective-action use (especially when they involve physical injuries). If security personnel don't have faith in their organization's protective-action evaluation process, they become unproductive, leading to decreases in personal and organizational safety.

The 1989 U.S. Supreme court decision in *Graham v. Connor*[4] codified what police officers knew for years preceding the decision: A hindsight use-of-force standard is unfair. Although this court decision doesn't directly apply to private personnel, the courts' rationale does. The court ruled what seems obvious to anyone employed in a vocation in which they're responsible for dealing with uncooperative, dangerous, and violent individuals: Field decision making is much more complicated than office decision making!

Policies and procedures for interacting with potentially violent individuals cannot be completely or perfectly defined. Therefore, it's unfair to apply a hindsight standard to security personnel use-of-force decision making.

From a business perspective, it's understandable that organizations would be reluctant to implement both situational use- of-force policies and a situational after-action review process. On one hand, this situational approach may seem to place employers in an impossible position for holding personnel accountable for their protective actions. On the other hand, it's unethical for organizations to create unrealistic standards against which to measure their personnel's actions. No matter how difficult it may be for organizations to find the proper balance between productivity and liability protection, organizations need to hold their security personnel accountable to both a fair use-of-force standard and a fair after-action evaluation process.

The Role of Review Boards in Accountability

Depending on the type and kind of subject interaction, it may be appropriate to utilize a protective-action review board to conduct an inquiry into the incident. Personnel who use protective action must justify and document its use, and their actions need to be subject to a protective-action review process. This process should be a thorough assessment of the circumstances and outcome of the employee decision to take action. This process should *not* be punitive or a witch hunt. This after-action evaluation also affords organizations an opportunity to access the effectiveness of their personnel security training.

An after-action protective-action review process is necessary for creating the type of transparency that's necessary for developing organizational and community partnerships and demonstrating an organizational commitment to treating all community members, including resistant subjects, fairly.

---

[4] See Chapter 11 for a more detailed exposition on *Graham v. Connor*.

Summary

Security personnel accountability plays an important role in successful conflict resolution. To create the safest and most secure organizations, organizations need to gain the cooperation of the people they serve. Accountability ensures that the people who interact with security personnel are treated fairly while also providing a high level of confidence for security individuals who may need to use protective action to protect both organizational and community members.

RECOMMENDATIONS

1. Supervise and enforce the organization's approved protective-action policies.
2. Require personnel to provide a full accounting, both verbally and in writing, whenever personnel are involved in using protective action to resolve conflict.
3. Create a fair standard to measure personnel protective action choices.
4. Utilize a review board to ensure quality control for protective-action use.
5. Create a culture of personnel accountability.

Index